Environmental Activism by Design

Published by AR+D

Applied Research and Design Publishing, an imprint of ORO Editions.
Gordon Goff: Publisher

www.appliedresearchanddesign.com
info@appliedresearchanddesign.com

USA, EUROPE, ASIA, MIDDLE EAST, SOUTH AMERICA

Managing Editor: Kirby Anderson
Copy editing: Leora Visotzky and Heather Corcoran
Book Design: Pablo Mandel / CircularStudio
Typeset in TT Hoves and Lyon Text

10 9 8 7 6 5 4 3 2 1 First Edition

Library of Congress data available upon request.
World Rights: Available

ISBN: 978-1-954081-79-6

Color Separations and Printing: ORO Group Ltd.
Printed in China.

International Distribution:
www.appliedresearchanddesign.com/distribution

ORO Editions makes a continuous effort to minimize the overall carbon footprint of its publications. As part of this goal, ORO Editions, in association with Global ReLeaf, arranges to plant trees to replace those used in the manufacturing of the paper produced for its books. Global ReLeaf is an international campaign run by American Forests, one of the world's oldest nonprofit conservation organizations. Global ReLeaf is American Forests' education and action program that helps individuals, organizations, agencies, and corporations improve the local and global environment by planting and caring for trees.

All book proceeds received by the Gulf Coast DesignLab will be donated to local organizations that restore coastal wetlands and Gulf Coast prairies.

Coleman Coker and Sarah Gamble

Environmental Activism by Design

Foreword by Thomas Fisher
Afterword by Katie Swenson

APPLIED RESEARCH +DESIGN PUBLISHING

**"Stay away from anything
that obscures the place it is in.
There are no unsacred places;
there are only sacred places
and desecrated places."**

— Wendell Berry, a portion of stanza two of "How to Be a Poet"[1]

1 Wendell Berry, "How to Be a Poet," Poetry Foundation, https://www.poetryfoundation.org/poetrymagazine/poems/41087/how-to-be-a-poet, Accessed 16 Feb 2022.

TABLE OF CONTENTS

Environmentalists at Sea Rim State Park conducting their semi-annual bird count from the deck of FLOAT.
© Coleman Coker

FOREWORD

An Architecture of Sentient Beings

Thomas Fisher

I write these words as the U.N's 26th Conference of the Parties, the annual gathering of national leaders and environmental activists, just wrapped up its work in Glasgow, Scotland.[1] While the conference produced agreements on how to address some key environmental challenges, such as curbing deforestation and clamping down on methane emissions, COP26 also showed the generational divide that exists across the globe between mainly older, government officials and the youth who will inherit the environmental damage those officials and their predecessors have done. One sign of that divide: over 100,000 youth protested in the streets of Glasgow as the politicians inside the conference center prevaricated. Meanwhile, the health of the planet continues to plummet.

The lack of urgency on the part of those in power in the face of extreme weather events of all sorts can cause one to give up hope in humanity's long-term survivability. No other species depends as much as we do on so many other types of plants and animals in order for us to thrive, and as we harm them through our environmental negligence, we only harm ourselves—which may be the greatest paradox humanity faces. Never has there been a species more powerful than us, in terms of the knowledge we possess and the technology we deploy, and yet never has there been a species more reliant than us on the diversity of ecosystems that we continue to damage and more vulnerable to the climate change that we continue to cause. We are in the midst of what ecologists have dubbed the planet's sixth great extinction, and the first one caused by an earth-bound creature: us.[2] At the same time, we seemly ignore the possibility that one of species that we might cause to go extinct, through our own ignorance and carelessness, might be us.

In a situation like this, considering our responsibility to others—ethics—becomes not just an academic exercise but also a matter of life and death, to us as individuals and to humanity itself.[3] Ethics asks us to think about the common good as opposed to our personal self-interest, although that typically occurs within a context in which we assume the future of the species is secure. But we can no longer assume that, given the speed with which we are extinguishing the very species we depend on. Consider the loss of bees, which pollinate one third of humanity's food supply: without them, there will be fewer of us, and fewer of the other animals that also depend on the plants that bees pollinate, which means even less food for at least the meat eaters among us.[4]

This requires a new way of thinking about ethics and about how we steward both the natural and built environments we create. The ethicist Peter Singer offers some useful guidance here.[5] He argues that we need to judge the utility of our decisions based on their effect not just on other humans, but also on other animals, "sentient beings" as Singer calls them, who feel pleasure and pain as much as we do. And while plant life does not have the consciousness of animals, our well-being as sentient creatures depends upon the plant communities that they—and we—need in order to live. Singer has placed the classic utilitarian goal of creating the greatest good for the greatest number in a broader context and in a way that is well-suited to the environmental challenges we face, forcing us to ask who we must include in the greatest number when trying to do the greatest good. If we only include people in that calculation, we fail the utilitarian test, and end up harming the plants and animals whose numbers far exceed ours, and whose continued existence predicates our own.

Singer's ethical stance has had its share of controversy. It leads to the conclusion, for example, that we should all become vegetarians, since we do not have a right to kill other sentient beings, any more than we have a right to kill other people, in order to eat.[6] Many people, of course, ignore such qualms and continue to eat meat, which should not surprise us: our intelligence as a species also increases our capacity for self-defeating delusion and self-serving denial. Which may, in the end, be humanity's Achilles heel: for all of our power and prowess as a species, our penchant for placing blame anywhere else except on ourselves, the cause of most blameworthy activity, may yet prove to be our truly fatal flaw. Singer's ethics, instead, urges us to take responsibility for the consequences of our actions on all of the other species with whom we share this planet, and to recognize that doing so also has the greatest utility for us.

Singer's view of utilitarianism has equally controversial consequences for the built environment. Of all human activities, the construction and operation of buildings demands a tremendous expenditure of material, labor, and energy, with environmental impacts all along the supply chain and across the life of the structure. Buildings, of course, have great utility, sheltering us from the elements, securing us against harm, and providing us with the space we need to live. But rarely do architects include other species in calculating the utility of our built environment; rarely do we think about the other species that occupied a building site before we arrived, and rarely do we ask how we might provide habitat for them in the process of constructing it for ourselves. Nor do enough architects consider the social and environmental consequences of material choices or design decisions, especially on far-off places or on the people producing what we specify.

A student screws down the floor deck at **INHABIT** on Galveston Island.
© Andre Boudreaux

Students install roof joists for **FRAME**, an outdoor classroom at the Coastal Heritage Preserve.
© Coleman Coker

The Gulf Coast DesignLab

All of which makes the work of the Gulf Coast Design Lab (GCDL) so instructive – and so inspiring. The projects portrayed here show how an ethically responsible approach to architecture can also produce a beautiful body of work that keeps in mind "the whole," as Coleman Coker continually reminds his class.[7] Many schools of architecture have design-build courses, in which students construct the designs they create in class, and the GCDL work represents a high-quality version of that pedagogy. And the small-scale and pavilion-like projects that design-build courses typically produce in order to fit the semester timeframes of most academic schedules also characterizes the GCDL output.

The difference with the GCDL work lies in its ethical and environmental implications. Consider the way in which the projects in this book address their sites. From the perspective of Singer's utilitarianism, a building site may be ours to own in a financial and legal sense, but we do not own it from an ethical or moral point of view, since even the most seemingly desolate site already contains far more sentient beings than the likely number of human beings who will occupy it. That does not mean that people have no right to the site, but it does mean that we have a responsibility in our treatment of it to accommodate the other animals with whom we share it, as the GCDL projects do.

In the project called FLOAT, the students created a structure that not only preserves the wetland in which it glides, but also creates an environmentally friendly "toilet" and a platform on which people can pitch tents. FLOAT creates a "site" for people to occupy without disrupting its actual, watery site.[8] Another GCDL project, called RISE, minimizes its impact on the site by using concrete pier

As part of their service-learning work, students from STORE help with native grass seedlings meant to re-establish coastal prairie areas on Galveston Island. © Ava Kikusaki

footings, which greatly reduce site excavation, while protecting this coastal project from rising tides.[9] And the project called INHABIT goes one step further, not only by supporting the structure on concrete piers, which allows animals to live below the platform floor, but also by creating a gabion wall of recycled concrete that provides occupiable space for small animals, with a surface area larger than the footprint of the structure itself.[10] Ideally, all architecture would do the same, increasing the habitable space for all of the creatures on a site, human and non-human alike.

The GCDL projects also show a deep understanding of the context in which they stand. Unlike other university based, design-build courses, where students and faculty often build projects quickly, with relatively little time for community engagement, the GCDL has had a long term relationship with the Gulf Coast communities in which it works. That represents not only a different approach to community based work, but also a different take on architectural practice. Mainstream practice has become one in which most architects move from one community and client to the next, designing buildings based on the firm's expertise and reputation, but with few long-term relationships with the people in each place. Architects, in some sense, have become a kind of invasive species, often creating designs for some far-off place, using products and materials from all over the country or the world, and specifying technology meant to insulate the occupants of buildings from changing outdoor conditions.

The GCDL suggests a very different approach to architecture. The structures it creates remain open to the surrounding landscape, providing shade and a degree of shelter from the elements, but without any interior, air-conditioned space. And when a project does create a space, like the "living room" in COOP, it has screen walls to keep out the bugs and let in the breeze and the view essential to the bird

Students from **SHIFT** help re-establish oyster beds in Galveston Bay as a way to help offset further beach erosion. © Ava Kikusaki

observation work of the people who gather there under its wing-like roof.[11] Or in the project called FRAME, the enclosure consists of full-height mosquito netting that people can pull back like curtains or unfurl as translucent drapes.[12]

Such examples remind us that, for most of human history, indigenous people - especially those in more temperate climates—conducted most of their activities outdoors, seeking shelter mainly at night or during inclement weather. Architecture as we now know it has moved most of those activities indoors, into buildings specifically designed for particular functions, while treating the outdoors mainly as a space through which we travel from one building to another. The GCDL work shows, instead, what a return to a more indigenous existence might involve, with minimal, permanent structures to provide some protection from the elements, but also able to accommodate a wide range of human activity, with each community deciding for itself what that might entail.

The indigenous nature of these structures goes beyond their open, flexible forms. Indigenous communities along bodies of water, like the Gulf of Mexico, often lived inland on higher ground, while constructing temporary structures near the coast, knowing that storms might blow them away. The GCDL projects embrace that strategy. In the project called STORE, for example, it has an open structure for the storage of kayaks that allows storm surges to pass right through the building.[13] And in the project called SHIFT, an open pavilion for collaborative work has columns, walls, and a roof that look as if a storm surge had already moved them from their original location.[14] These projects may not look indigenous, given their use of modern materials, like concrete and steel, and their aesthetic of planar walls and roofs that reflect a modern sensibility. But in practice, these projects act indigenously in their embrace of impermanence and in their openness to unpredictability.

Indigenous communities left little architecture behind for the archaeological record, because most did not think of the structures they inhabited as permanent, and the same is true of the other sentient beings with whom we share this planet. Like the animal kingdom, of which we are a part, humanity has, for most its history, lived in temporary shelter, constructed from the materials available at hand. Only in the last 5% of our history as a species did we start to build permanent settlements, with structures on fixed foundations, and only in the last 1% of our history did we develop architecture of the sort we now study in architecture school.[15]

Which suggests the following question: What if architecture as we have come to know it is an aberration, a temporary detour along the road to resilience for our species? Such a question may seem like heresy coming from a professor in a school of architecture, but the health of any discipline depends upon its willingness to challenge its most basic assumptions. Humans, like every other sentient being, requires physical protection of some sort, so shelter will remain a fundamental need of ours. But does that shelter have to take the form it has, especially over the last century, as buildings have become increasingly specialized in terms of their function and increasingly artificial in terms of their interior conditions.

What if, as Singer might say, we did not just consider the interests of other animal species in our decisions, but learned from them and even appropriated their survival strategies as our own? The GCDL projects offer one model of what that might be like. Every other sentient being on the planet builds its shelter with locally available materials, most of it in a temporary fashion, and human beings did much the same for most of our history, with minimal shelter for the family or tribal group and with most activities happening outdoors, in collective and collaborative efforts.

The GCDL projects pointedly avoid the construction of housing or even shelter in the sense of a private enclosure. Instead, the GCDL has produced a series of public spaces and structures for people to gather and to seek shade from the sun, places to sit, and protection from mosquitoes. This is not an architecture of private self-interest, but one of public life and collaborative engagement, for people to come in order to participate in the activities that make us most human, as one of the most sociable of sentient beings. The GCDL work suggests a possible future much like our distant past, in which people lived in small, and somewhat temporary shelters, while gathering to work, learn, or play in meaningful places.

From the perspective of Peter Singer, that would align with the way in which every other sentient being lives. Most other animals do not wait to get flooded out by a storm or burned out by a firestorm; instead, they migrate. We humans like to think of ourselves as smarter and cleverer than the other species with whom we share the planet. But climate change—and COVID-19—have shown how short-sighted and confused we really are as we continue to engage in the very things that threaten us the most. Were we truly smart and clever, we would ask not what buildings to build, but instead, do we need buildings at all, and if so, how little can we build to meet our needs without neglecting those who already live in a place or who may live there in the future? That is an architectural question, but as Singer's work suggests, it is also an ethical question, and ultimately a social and environmental one as well.

Endnotes

1 United Nations, COP26 (https://ukcop26.org/).
2 Elizabeth Kolbert, *The Sixth Extinction, An Unnatural History* (New York: Henry Holt, 2014).
3 Thomas Fisher, *Architectural Design and Ethics, Tools for Survival* (Oxford: Architectural Press, 2008).
4 John Haltiwanger, "If All The Bees In The World Die, Humans Will Not Survive," *Elite Daily*, September 15, 2014 (https://www.elitedaily.com/news/world/humans-need-bees-to-survive/755737).
5 Peter Singer, *Writings on an Ethical Life* (New York: Ecco Press, 2000).
6 Peter Singer. *Animal Liberation* (New York: Harper Collins, 1975).
7 Coleman Coker, "Act as If Your House is on Fire," *Environmental Activism by Design* (San Francisco: Applied Research and Design Publishing", 2022).
8 Ibid, p. 46.
9 Ibid, p. 58.
10 Ibid. p. 70.
11 Ibid. p. 120.
12 Ibid. p. 154.
13 Ibid. p. 110.
14 Ibid. p. 132.
15 Yuval Noah Harari, Sapiens, *A Brief History of Humankind* (New York: Harper, 2014).

To get a better understanding of the ecological conditions in which they'll work, students from DUNE spend the beginning of their semester exploring the local landscape on Mustang Island.
© Coleman Coker

Introduction

Coleman Coker and Sarah Gamble

Environmental Activism by Design developed over several years of reflection and writing, taking shape as both documentation and dialogue about the Gulf Coast DesignLab, its process, and the fundamental questions it poses for architectural education and professional practice. We both experienced the impact of Hurricane Katrina firsthand—its effects increased by climate change—while working at New Orleans's Tulane University in the years following the storm, and it was made abundantly clear that climate-change related disasters and social inequity concerns were two sides of the same coin. Our Texas-based collaboration emerged from an initial article in *Texas Architect* about the GCDL project FLOAT and grew to become a publication that celebrates and interrogates the first decade of GCDL's work and our profession's trajectory.

This book is truly co-authored, with chapters written from an insider's perspective (Coker as GCDL director, who teaches and leads the program at the University of Texas at Austin) and from an onlooker's vantage point (Gamble as researcher and former UT Austin faculty, who has remained actively interested in GCDL's process and impact). Developing the publication was a learning process for us both, spurred by internal conversations and our belief in the potential of GCDL's approach to impact how designers learn about, and engage in, the environment around them. While we would both describe ourselves as Public Interest Design practitioners and are committed to supporting the next generation of PID, our contrasting writing styles and chapter content captures our differing generational perspectives (Baby Boomer and Xennial) and areas of focus within the developing field.

Environmental Activism by Design acknowledges the complex challenges faced by coastal communities and our professional responsibility to aid in their pursuit of environmental justice and resilience. Within the book, you'll find a specific focus

Students from **SHIFT** cut sheet steel for screens that lend privacy to an adjoining neighborhood.
© Coleman Coker

Students from **PARTING WALLS** survey the area where they will soon work, looking for clues that can lead to an appropriate design.
© Coleman Coker

on Texas, exploring the Gulf Coast through the themes of place, poetics, ethics, and action. The publication takes the form of four chapter essays, with alternating authors, punctuated by four pairs of completed projects explored through large format images, line drawings, and project overviews. These eight projects were selected from the over twenty-five total projects completed by GCDL students for the collective range of project types, mix of clients and users, and design excellence. Within the book, GCDL projects are highlighted in the project catalog and visually located on a map of the Texas coast. Additional information can be found on GDCL's website (www.gulfcoastdesignlab.org).

Going beyond our words, the publication interweaves the voices of others. Reflections from GDCL alumni, drawn from one-on-one interviews and responses to an open-ended online questionnaire, capture their experiences in the program and its impact on their education and practice. Alumnus Joseph Hernandez succinctly sums up much of what the GCDL program sets out to instill in its students when he described what he learned by working on OBSERVE in 2018 as "emphasizing how design can add to and focus on nature rather than replace or obscure it."[1] Interviews with project clients are similarly highlighted, providing the perspectives of GCDL collaborators engaged in the life and health of the Gulf Coast on a daily basis. In his Foreword, Thomas Fisher, former dean of the University of Minnesota School of Architecture and thought leader in Public Interest Design and professional ethics, points us in the direction we aspire to take with the book by voicing his concern about our world leaders' lack of commitment to the necessary change required to offset the climate disaster, which Fisher then compares with ethicist Peter Singer's call for interspecies equality. In closing, Katie Swenson, Principal at MASS (Model of Architecture Serving Society) and longtime leader of Enterprise's Rose Fellowship, calls us into action with her passionate contribution.

Environmental Activism by Design explores the reasons why our work focuses on the Gulf Coast of Texas. After all, it's a minimum three-hour drive from our campus in Austin. That requires us to take multiple trips each semester, to rent trucks for shipping components prefabricated on campus, to coordinate carpooling and student lodging, and to offset the carbon footprint of our travel. There are certainly outstanding opportunities closer to campus where students could find meaningful design investigation. But the "black gold" coast of Texas is unlike any other place, where the shadow of the petrochemical industry looms large, its products—ones we all use—generating an overabundance of greenhouse gases and pollution that wreak havoc on local ecologies—vitally important topics that begin each semester's work. Dynamic change from climatic events—hurricanes, seasonal storms with heavy rains—can take place in a semester's time, offering students the opportunity to study those transformations as they happen. Social inequity is rife along the Gulf Coast because of the immense wealth gap from some of the world's richest robber-barons whose global corporations are headquartered there, extracting profit and leaving pollution behind. The Gulf Coast exemplifies our unfolding climate disaster, foreshadowed in its sensitive ecosystem's collision with neoliberal economics. Environmental injustice is rampant there too, because the state has some of the most lax environmental protection policies in the country. Any of these conditions alone would make a place unique and provide a dynamic laboratory for learning, but when combined, they deliver an unparalleled opportunity to discuss their impact and the role design might play in mitigating some of their long-term harms.

With this place as our students' classroom—one vast and living field station for applied research—its ever-shifting character might be best described as a forever-morphing, weird cyborg-like creature, its skeletal structure wrought of oil rigs, refineries, underground oil and gas pipe, and its "flesh" a life-filled "natural" ecology mixed with a rich social structure that somehow finds a way to coexist. The book describes this incongruous mix and how it creates a dynamic *ecotone* where difference collides, comingles, and integrates into a matchless interdependent vibrancy—not necessarily equal, not always pretty, but nonetheless conjoined. Its complexities and sometimes head-scratching contradictions are extravagant, offering a more than fertile ground for design exploration.

The first chapter, "Red Tide, Red Necks and Littoral Drift," examines several of these concerns in detail, focusing on the fact that the Texas coast—like all coastal zones around the world—is increasingly suffering from the impacts of increasing sea level rise, morphed weather patterns, rising pollution, escalating overdevelopment, accelerating habitat loss, rapid erosion of its beaches and bays, and subsidence. It considers how these factors shape the GCDL's approach of actualized pragmatism to teaching design students. Getting off campus and into this multifaceted field, students come face-to-face with many of the same ecological problems humanity faces worldwide; at the same time, they encounter complex social issues that play out over much of the planet. Just about every critical issue facing our world today is condensed into this relatively thin strip of sandy coastline, providing a unique opportunity for young designers. As Chapter One maintains, the Gulf Coast is a magnifying glass that brings into focus the rapid global change brought about by planet-wide ecological shifts, a locale where students encounter a critical patient in need of immediate triage. With its

A CULTIVATE student listens to residents from the neighborhood in which she and her fellow students will design and build their project.
© Ava Kikusaki

swift change and immense challenges, the Gulf Coast can feel like an emergency room environment into which GCDL students get thrown.

With these concerns at the forefront, much of the book centers on DesignLab students' charge to reimagine architecture as a medium, not just about form-making aesthetics, but about ethical *action* as well. Aesthetically pleasing places are indeed important—and we believe you'll see that the student's work confirms that—but the book argues that beauty is not enough in today's world of social and environmental meltdown. Likewise, the GCDL is more than an exercise in designing and building places for the public; throughout the book you'll find examples of students learning through less-conventional means than found in traditional architectural pedagogy, where "ethics-in-action" work includes getting waist-deep in brackish waters to help reestablish oyster reefs, working with non-profits to plant native grasses that regenerate coastal prairies, planting live oaks in state parks, and picking up trash in sensitive wetland habitats. This goes beyond making the place in which they are designing ecologically stronger; it also draws students closer to understand it more deeply. The resulting designs are not only appropriate, they become part of the ecology of the locale itself.

Chapter Two, "A Model for Learning: The Gulf Coast DesignLab," provides a detailed overview of the GCDL program, breaking its approach down into seven sections. It is intended to provide a replicable model for architectural practice and education that is adaptable to local conditions. Reflections from GCDL clients and alumni bring a range of voices into the chapter, allowing personal experiences to shape GCDL's story over the past decade. Technical discussions of budget, materiality, schedule, and logistics all point back to the program's focus

Students on board the M/V Sam Houston examine first-hand the massive petrochemical industry along Houston's Ship Channel.
© Coleman Coker

on environmental education and the goal of fostering respect for the natural environment throughout the process. On the Gulf Coast, these future designers have the opportunity to recognize that what they learn there can be applied to the many other places on the planet that they will one day help shape.

The third essay, "Act As If Your House Is On Fire," describes how GCDL students come to the place they work with the goal of making a difference. *Environmental Activism by Design* explores their contributions toward a healthier coastal environment through their ongoing research of social and ecological concerns, as well as their design-build efforts that provide well-constructed and inspiring structures where others teach and train the public about the environment and how to better protect it. And while the book highlights these projects in detail, the drive of the GCDL, like life, is all about the trip taken and not the destination; it is less about the products that students design and build, but instead a process that offers room for growth in becoming astute and compassionate designers. *Environmental Activism by Design* examines the importance of ethical forethought in an architect's work, exemplified in instances when students visit fenceline communities of color that back up to petrochemical facilities. There they meet residents coping with the fact that they and their children are exposed daily to more toxic chemicals than are allowed in most other states, making them statistically sicker than those in the more affluent neighborhood just a few miles away. Students, who themselves come from a range of backgrounds, including communities facing similar challenges, quickly come to understand that those families live there not by choice, but out of necessity, highlighting the fact that environmental injustice is often tied to economic disparity and skin color. The book describes how investigations such as these allow GCDL students to better understand their own ethical responsibilities—maybe for the first time—with their minds *and* with their hearts.

Chapter Four, "A Responsibility to Place," discusses the importance of designers learning to think on a global scale through better understanding the local complexities of place. The chapter compels educators and the profession alike to consider alternative ways to teach and practice that reflect deeply on the ecology—social and natural—of the place in which they teach and work. And, through that reflection, find respect and even reverence. This is exemplified through the participatory research documented in the book's many photographs: students walking the beach or hiking coastal prairie trails, witnessing waterfowl and sea life exist side-by-side with the ever-sprawling gated communities that elbow each other out for a glimpse of the ocean, kayaking in bay waters as looming refineries fill the horizon as far as the eye can see. These experiences drive home that they are at ground zero of one of the largest petrochemical manufacturing complexes in the world. These experiences offer pause, allowing students to reflect on how their more-thorough understanding of a place through experience will better shape their work. Taking it all in, the book describes how GCDL students begin to recognize the hard truth that the health of the coast has been sacrificed for the short-term gains that oil, gas, and chemical production deliver, something they may not have given much thought to before. It is a place where they quickly realize that many of the problems we face as a society have no answers when approached with conventional architectural thinking, forcing many of our students to reconsider their fundamental understanding of architecture.

These first four chapters contend that getting out of the classroom and into the world challenges the idealized architecture many students may be used to pursuing—at least the way it's often depicted in design schools as a pleasing, equitable context full of designer buildings where people with "taste" want to live. When face-to-face with the contradictions and vitality that is the coast, students realize they are about as far from the fantasy of heroic architecture as one can get. Yet some find an unexpected energy to it all—a kind of horrific beauty, a Mad Max–meets–Wizard of Oz aesthetic of industrial materials and buildings on stilts

Bird enthusiasts look out over the wetlands from OBSERVE, the Oppenheimer Bird Observatory on Galveston Island.
© Mary Warwick

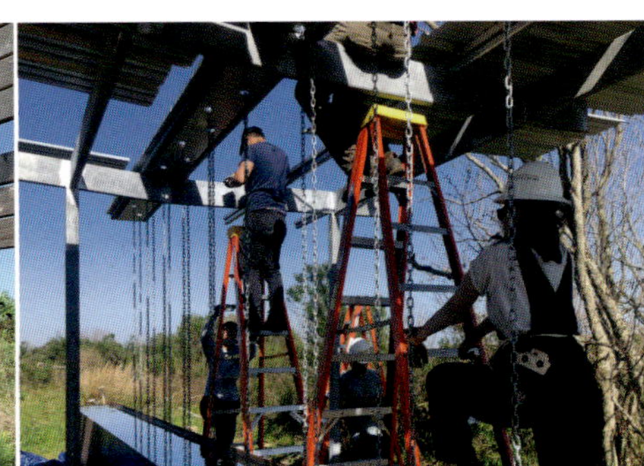

Students install a gutter and rain chains over the native plants aquatic garden at SUSTAIN, a new field station for K-8th grade kids at Crenshaw School for Environmental Studies in Port Bolivar, TX.
© Coleman Coker

that has a dark attraction, and is evidence of the resilience of the human spirit even in the most extreme contexts. Much like the GCDL studio itself, the book highlights these insights by discussing the glaring differences of wealth, class, environmental injustice, and inequity that are out in the open for students to witness. Students see that, just like the health and vitality of the "natural" environment, these human factors hang in the balance between corporate greed and societal need. In this post-industrial, post-nature, post-human culture, the book depicts how the "dirty coast" is a place where students' untested ideals about design are challenged, where an expanded possibility for architecture's potential might be realized through a new kind of ecological thinking.

If your heart is not breaking by what is happening to the earth, it is because you don't yet understand the magnitude of the harm we are doing. Once you become mindful of the impact we're having, you can either sink into grief-stricken hopelessness or you can take that sorrow and turn it into an expression of hope by working to change what's causing the devastation. No matter how small, committing to help better the world is the most courageous thing you'll ever do. Courage is necessary for all of us if we are to honestly face this existential threat and admit we are the problem. Courage is essential if we want to step out of our comfort zone and commit to making a better world. It is from this standpoint of knowledgeable activism, that the book's conclusion, "Ripples of Hope," reveals its core concept: This book is really about you, the reader. Highlighting the outstanding work of over three-hundred-and-fifty GCDL students, we hope to inspire you, to motivate, and hearten you. If you are not already steadfast and working to make the world just a little bit better for yourself and others, we believe the work of our students will encourage you to do just that, to make a difference, no matter how large or small. *Environmental Activism by Design* asks you to open yourself to the world and bear witness to the beauty and complexity that is all around. Experience it and embrace it, just like many of our students have, with fresh eyes and an open heart. Whether educator, practitioner, student or someone simply interested in imaginative pragmatism, you will find this world can be an extraordinary place providing everything you desire. It offers drop-to-your-knees beauty that fills our spirits, and it's telling us now, more than ever, that it needs our love, hope, and respect. Once you find *your* relationship with it—see, smell, hear, touch, and taste the all-encompassing quality of all that it is—we're convinced you'll be encouraged to take a little better care of this earth and all the living souls that depend on it. This is the desire we have for you in writing this book. Know that you can make a difference.

Endnotes

1 Joseph Hernandez, (IHNABIT, Summer 2018), Response to GCDL Alumni Questionnaire, 27 September 2021.

Students discuss the potential ecological impacts of their design for DUNE in Port Aransas, TX. © Coleman Coker

Students relax at GATHER at Goose Island State Park on the Lamar Peninsula. © Coleman Coker

View looking up through the way-finding tower of FLOAT in Sea Rim State Park's wetlands preserve near Port Arthur, TX.
© Coleman Coker

Projects Catalogue

The project catalogue highlights each of the twenty-nine projects undertaken by Gulf Coast DesignLab students over the past ten years. Listed in chronological order, each project entry highlights the names of participating students and teaching assistants (when applicable), paired with the client name and project location. Each of the twenty-six Texas projects is physically located on a corresponding project map, which can be found on the inner fold of this book's back cover.

Each project is given a unique name. These names are collectively determined by the students and the outcome of an exercise given early on in the semester, prior to the start of their design work. While on-site for the first time, the students are asked to find a place to sit quietly and alone for twenty minutes (no earbuds, please) to reflect on what they are sensing. Using all their senses—not just sight—they are asked to make notes of their experiences, and then, to arrive at five action words that capture their reflections. (Occasionally, this assignment will be accompanied by an additional sketch exercise, a mechanism to further concentration on their locale and begin to build a relationship with it.) Toward the end of the studio's design phase and when they are heavily invested in their project direction, each student is asked to select an action word that describes the chief active characteristic of their design. Once chosen, the students share their words, which are then discussed by the group as a way to find commonality of intent. From these shared words, the students select a name—typically one word but not exclusively—on which they can all agree describes what the project sets out to do. The outcome of this process are names such as CULTIVATE, MOVE, HIDE, FRAME, DEMONSTRATE and SUSTAIN, each with the intent of conveying a design idea through the power of words.

01 **PARTING WALLS**

Fall 2012 | South Texas Botanical Gardens and Nature Center | Corpus Christi, TX
Project Team: Elizabeth deRegt, Laura Edwards, Wilson Hack, Jena Hammond, Jon Handzo, Jaclyn Hensy, Jessica Painter, Molly Purnell, David Schneider, Greg Street, Tristan Walker. © Coleman Coker

02 **BLIND SIDED**

Spring 2013 | University of Texas Marine Science Institute | Port Aransas, TX
Project Team: Timothy Campbell, Todd Ferry, Garland Fielder, Matt Krolick, Jon Mautz, Lauren Mullane, Annie Palone, Katherine Russett, Jessica Zarowitz. © Coleman Coker

03 **PORTAL**

Summer 2013 | City of Austin Parks and Recreation Department | Austin, TX
Project Team: Catherine Berry, Ana Calhoun, Brittany Cooper, Alessandra Figueiredo, Nicole Joslin, Cameron Kraus, Tran Hoang Le, Andrea Lewis, Jordan Teitelbaum, Riley Uecker, Carrie Waller | Teaching Assistant: Conner Bryan. © Coleman Coker

04 **EXPANDED FIELD**

Summer 2013 | City of Austin Parks and Recreation Department | Austin, TX
Project Team: Casey-Marie Claude, John Cunningham, Kelly Denker, Brian Gaudio, Anna Katsios, Gordon Lee, Matthew Martinec, Marianne Nepsund, Nathaniel Schneider, Daniel Sebaldt, Allison Stoos | Teaching Assistant: Conner Bryan. © Coleman Coker

05 **HEAVY WATER**

Fall 2013 | Museum of Old and New Art (MONA) | Hobart, Tasmania, Australia
Project Team: Shelby Blessing, Danuta Dias, Shelley Evans, Andrew Houston, Lauren Jones, Kye Killian, Alex Krippner, Jorge Martinez Jr, Morgan Parker, Mitch Peterson, David Sharratt, Katie Summers. © Morgan Parker, 1 © Coleman Coker, 2-3

06 **DUNE**

Spring 2014 | The University of Texas Marine Science Institute | Port Aransas, TX
Project Team: Peter Binder, Sara Fallahi, Jorge Faz, Kimberly Harding, Christina Hunter, Yinrui Li (Nicholas), Barron Peper, Ryan Rasmussen, Shelby Sickler.
© Coleman Coker

07 **CULTIVATE**

Summer 2014 | City of Austin Redevelopment Department | East Side Ally - Austin, TX
Justin Bell, Ann Charleston, Kathleen Clark, Katy Coyne, Elizabeth Farrell, Justin Fleury, Biying Kong, Eric Melville, Daniel Montaivo, April Ng, Mark Nordby, Kaethe Selkirk, Claire Simpson, Sarah Wassel. © Thomas Johnston, 1 © Coleman Coker, 2-3

08 **GATHER**

Fall 2014 | Goose Island State Park | Lamar Peninsula, TX
Project Team: Rachel Duggan, Katherine Eastman, Jamie Epley, Huiming Zuo (Zoe), Thomas Johnston, Kuan Liu, Celine Pinto, Ruihua Cai (Mark), Luke Stevenson, Teng Li (James). © Luke Stevenson, 1 © Coleman Coker, 2-3

09 **VANAKKAM**

Spring 2015 | Bodhidharma School | Aleyendal Village | Tamil Nadu, India
Project Team: Rebecca Brown, Felipe Calderon, Pearlene Cheah, Alex Dallas, Ricardo Diaz, Joel Effland, Siwen Fang, Angeliki Giannisi, Tobias Gutheil, Claire Miller, Ben Parker, Alex. © Aimée Toledano

10 **MOVE**

Summer 2015 | Public Interest Design Studio | Green Gate Farms – Austin, TX
Project Team: Jeffery Elliott, Kristen Fulmer, Laney Gorman, Amy Grossman, Joyce Hanlon, Kara Holekamp, Andrew Horne, Andrew Kao, Hanqi Li, Shuo Li, Sean O'Brien, Alison Steele, Taylor Stumberg, Jordan Teitelbaum, Noah Winkler, Quan (Vanilla), Yin. © Alison Steele, 1-3 © Coleman Coker, 2

11 **CANOPY**

Fall 2015 | Goose Island State Park | Lamar Peninsula, TX
Project Team: Kristen Ericson, Kamree Gonzales, Ashley Harris, Sean Kennaugh, Drew McMillian, Cory Olsen, Denis, Piereschi, Cristopher Salazar, Dominic Sargeant, Stuart Yancey. © Alison Steele, 1-3 © Coleman Coker, 2

12 **FLOAT**

Spring 2016 | Sea Rim State Park | Sabine Pass, TX
Project Team: Nevin Blum, Michelle Cantu, Connie Chang, Claire Fontaine, Evan Greulich, Asher Intebi, Marissa Jordan, Estrella Juarez, Kelsey Kaiser, Kevin Keating, Amy McDonnold, Ashley Nguyen, Raquel. © Kelsey Kaiser, 1 © Coleman Coker, 2-3

13 **HIDE**

Summer 2016 | Camp Aranzazu | Red Fish Point on Copano Bay – Fulton, TX
Project Team: Charles Beckendorf, Kuan-Ying Chiu, Luke Kvasnicka, Li Xinmei, Eric Mattson, Daniel Montalvo, Adolfo Moreno, Sara Ramirez, Joel Sterling, Allison Walvoord, Amy Witte | Teaching Assistant: Josh Leger. © Aldolfo Moreno, 1 © Coleman Coker, 2-3

14 **RISE**

Fall 2016 | Goose Island State Park | Lamar Peninsula, TX
Project Team: Eric Alexander, Sara Bensalem, Mitch Flora, Hannah Frossard, James Holliday, Hannah Ivancie, Josh Leger, Max Mahaffey, Ola Olakunie, Qianhui Miao (Vonn), Michelle Sifre, Sebastian Rojas Sonderegger, Neive Tierney. © Max McHaffey, 1 © Coleman Coker, 2-3

15 **STORE**

Spring 2017 | Coastal Heritage Preserve | Galveston Island, TX
Project Team: Ryan Carlisle, Emily Chaney, Clayton Cain, Sadie Dubicki, Samantha Gutteridge, Haley Lovelady, Chloe Malek, Marsden Merkle, Renica Naeva, Marriene Ondo, Alexandra Padila, Anjulie Palta, Julie Patterson, Ian Randall, Yee (Fiona) Sang Wong. © Pia Navarrete Garcia, 1 © Coleman Coker, 2-3

16 **INHABIT**

Summer 2017 | Galveston Island State Park | Galveston Island, TX
Project Team: Andrea Becker, Andre Boudreaux, Brooke Burnside, Avignon Greene, Rebecca Kennedy, Whitney Moore, Hugo Reynolds, Sean Reynolds, Joey Rocha, Ui Jun Song, Anthony Vannette | Teaching Assistant: Patrick Schoonover. © Avi Greene, 1-3 © Coleman Coker, 2

17 **RECOVER**

Fall 2017 | Post-Harvey Recovery and Relief | Impacted Communities on the Texas Coast
Project Team: Bradley Jury, Jennifer Lyssy, Brenden Murphy, A J Stedman, Sydney Ritter Stedman, Hannah Williams, Robyn Wrobleski | A special thanks to the more than forty students not part of this studio who volunteered their time to help restore parts of the Texas Gulf Coast devastated by Hurricane Harvey. © Coleman Coker

18 **FRAME**

Spring 2018 | Coastal Heritage Preserve | Galveston Island, TX
Project Team: Pei Wei Chang, Maria Pia Navarrete Garcia, Maggie Gaudio, Danlin Huang, Iyengar Sudarshan, Reuben Joesph, Miguel Rodriguez, Jordah Sheets, Derek Smith, Andrew Stone, Brandon Tharp, Claire Townley, Angela Vanella. © Coleman Coker

19 **ARRIVE**

Summer 2018 | Camp Aranzazu | Rockport, TX
Project Team: Helena Aguirre, Delaney Bannister, Hailey Brown, King Fai (Kim) Choy, Andrew Garden, Annie Liu, Elizabeth Matos, Elijah Montez, Diego Zubizarreta. © Coleman Coker

20 **OBSERVE**

Fall 2018 | Coastal Heritage Preserve | Galveston Island, TX
Project Team: Jacob Castine, Alejandro Davilla, Micayla Garza, Joseph Hernandez, Aaron McMurry, (Fiona) Yee Sang Wong, Zichao XU. © Coleman Coker

21 **YUCATAN**

Spring 2019 | Laguna Rosado Ecological Habitat | Merida and Puerto Progresso, Mexico
Project Team: Melissa Chen, Rachel Deschner, Guadalupe Suarez, Sydney Galloso, Ellis Kaufmann, Maryam Quraishi, Saisha Rayala, Jacob Reed, Hannah Saji, Derek Smith, Caroline Tate, Alexandra Wilkinson. © Coleman Coker

22 **SHIFT**

Summer 2019 | Galveston Bay Foundation | Kemah, TX
Project Team: Stephanie Almendares, Daniel Aronson, Nai'lah Bell-Eden, David Burns, Arlene Ellwood, Catherine Kanter, Brandon Lawry, Amaya Lucas, Harrison Marek, Lena Page, Tyler Schuertz, Shelby Taubenkimel, Inci Uckok, Alex Uhlmann, Ariella Yendler. | Teaching Assistant: Andrew Garden. © Coleman Coker

23 **COOP**

Fall 2019 | Houston Audubon Society | High Island, TX
Project Team: Natalie Avellar, Luis Bosquez, Marcella Pastrano, Christian Pena, Draven Pointer, Makayla Ponce, Trenton Sexton, McKenzie Sosa, Iuliia Tambovtseva, Valentina Tambovtseva, Emrehan Tuna, Ruofeng You. © Coleman Coker

24 **BRIDGE**

Spring 2020 & Spring 2021 | Houston Audubon Society | High Island, TX
Project Team: Wellington Chew, Bernadette Cole, Hannah George, Christie Johnson, Laura Marley Lancaster, Kate Leyendecker, Abby Lopez, Makayla Rutt, Lan (Joanne) Zhou, Brandt Hanson for the generous donation of his time. © Coleman Coker

25 **DEMONSTRATE**

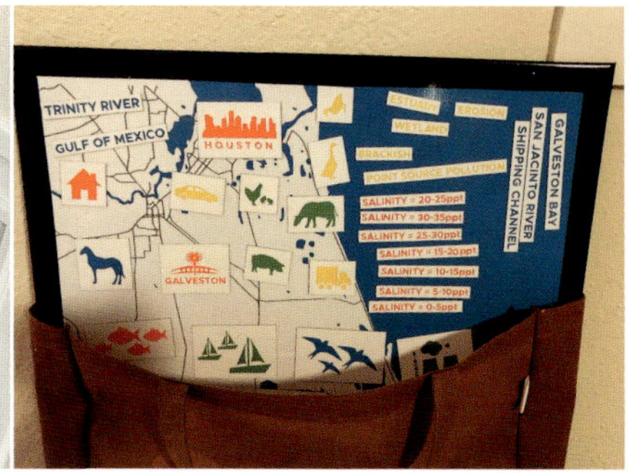

Summer 2020 | Artist Boat on behalf of Houston Area K -12 Public Schools | Houston, TX
Project Team: Tristan Ahiquist, Kate Bomar, Cara Bristow, Susie Gibson, Matthew Hodges, Lyndsey Howarth, Annie Jenkins, Danielle Koplitz, Lucy Lloyd, Gabrielle Maudlin, Maggie McKenna, Alexander St Angelo, Avery Tenorio, Charles Weber, II, Leah Wyatt. © Karissa Laffey, 1 © Ava Kikusaki, 2 © Gabrielle Maudlin

26 **SIMULATE**

Fall 2020 | Armand Bayou Nature Center | Houston, TX
Project Team: Leesa Cano, Kalie Currin, Chandler Householder, Maggie Laird, Bennett Lembcke, Rose Li, Omar McClung, Alex McKenzie, Meaghan Pensacola-Rouchon, Trelyn Patterson, Michael West, Courtney Williams. © Coleman Coker

27 **RESTORE I & II**

Spring & Summer 2021 | Ecology Action at Circles Acres | Austin, TX
Project Team (Spring): Lauren Boyd, Victoria Carter, Fernando Davila, Amaya Dsouza, Jessica (Guppy) Go, John Katada, Alex Kelley, Cameron Leigh, Bobby Nolen, Nicole Raskosky, Blair Stingley, Charley Tyeskie, Abigail Winfield, Cameron Young | (Summer): Adam Bell, Kaavya Chhatrapati, Justin Perkins, Amy Rojas, Kevin Tsao. © Coleman Coker

28 **SUSTAIN**

Fall 2021 | Crenshaw School for Environmental Studies | Port Bolivar, TX
Project Team: Marina Avina, Stefan Brits, Alfredo Corona, Emily Dauskurdas, Jonathan Malott, Chi-Shen Ni, Melannie Ruiz, Zein Tao. © Coleman Coker

29 **IGNITE**

Spring 2022 | Girl Scouts San Jacinto Council | Galveston TX
Project Team: Michael Anowey, Andrew Brandt, Joseph Chandler, Heather Corcoran, Alvar Favela-Ramos, Gabriel Friedstadt, Judy Labib, Curtis Lechner, Kassandra Lee, Taylor Luehr, Hannah Oppelt, Andre Rezaie, Max Vela. © Akiko Hamma

Students frame COOP's sun screen at the Houston Audubon Society's Coastal Operations Center on High Island. © Coleman Coker

Students from COOP take a break to enjoy morning views of the Gulf of Mexico.
© Ava Kikusaki

Redfish are one of the most sought-after fish on the Texas coast. This discarded head, along with a dozen others, was discarded along the highway in Port Aransas; some fisherperson had an excellent catch that day.
© Coleman Coker

CHAPTER 1

Red Tide, Red Necks and Littoral Drift

Coleman Coker

Aptly named, the Gulf Coast DesignLab works on the Gulf Coast of the Gulf of Mexico, specifically the Texas coast. For many, Texas does not conjure up images of long stretches of sandy beaches and pounding ocean surf. Yet, 367 miles (591 km) of the state face the sea, making it the sixth longest coastline in the United States. Unlike much of the overdeveloped US Gulf edge, a great deal of the Texas coast is rugged and undeveloped, much due to the coastline being protected by barrier islands. Padre Island, at 113-miles (182 km) long, is reportedly the longest barrier island in the world (some things in Texas really are bigger). Following are Mustang Island, San José Island, Matagorda Island, Greek Island, Egret Island, San Luis Island, Galveston Island, and the Bolivar Peninsula (an almost-island). These thin, sandy strips—rich habitats for birds, mammals, reptiles, sea-life, and everything else that gains sustenance where earth meets ocean—are the mainland's first line of defense against tropical storms and even deadlier hurricanes. Yet, like all barrier islands, they are in constant states of change. It is normal for oceanside beaches to disappear, reappear, disappear again, and end up somewhere else. Barrier islands are always shifting, always in flux. This age-old process is called littoral drift. Ongoing island drift is caused by tide and wind, particularly when island edges strike acute angles. Tides and wind pull sand from the ocean floor and beach edges, carrying it where the winds and waves take it. For centuries, the Texas Coast has been in transition like this, sculpted by wind and tides. Through the magic of dynamic equilibrium, barrier islands always change, yet they stay the same: thin slivers of sandy life morphing, reshaping, and regrouping—altered, yet, in their own way, constant.

These everchanging isles are increasingly impacted by our activity. And with populations on the Texas coast rapidly expanding—just like at most ocean edges around the world—developers and private property landowners, whose pocketbooks rely on stability, do what it takes to keep their investments intact. They—and most of us—feel that change shouldn't impact our lives or investments. We expect a sense of permanence in the places we choose to live, and we stubbornly fight the ebbs and flows of intertwined ecological change to maintain it. The artillery needed for this battle on the Gulf Coast comes in battalions of jetties, shielding sea walls, platoons of groynes marching out to sea, wave attenuators, and artificial islands. All have the same objective for victory: vanquishing the ever-shifting ocean edges. Like so many wars, these are campaigns that should never have been mounted, battles that cannot be won. And like most ill-planned conflicts, these maritime armies are reinforced by large allocations of funds that could be put to better use. But it's not just a waste of tax dollars; what's most damaging is the long-term collateral damage of ecological ruin. For example, beach nourishing, a heavy armament implement used in the war on change, is particularly devastating. Five-foot diameter pipes, reaching out from the shore for hundreds of yards, suck up the sand—and all the life it holds—from the ocean floor and pump it landward for new beach, replacing the beach that wandered off by the natural forces of littoral drift. The ecological damage this causes is high. A city like Galveston, for example, is forever armoring and re-nourishing its main economic engine, the beach, where it is common to see large steel pipes stretching along the water's edge. To the casual beachgoer, the sandy shore seems natural enough. But, in fact, it's as artificial as the twelve-foot concrete seawall that separates the beach from the miles of hotels, gas stations, and gift shops lining Galveston's seawall.

"In the GCDL I understood finally that social issues are inextricably linked to environmental ones. The truth can be terrifying and grotesque, but it's better to understand this to become motivated and passionate in life, to care deeply about climate change and equity concerns."
—Omar McClung, SIMULATE

Armored edges that keep these Disneyland-like beaches in place infer Never-Neverland permanence. From Port Isabel to Port Arthur, this false stability increasingly entices new, single-family-home owners and the subdivisions they fill. Acres of meticulously manicured lawns cover the McMansion yards—though these homes are raised on fifteen-foot-high stilts. Like artificial green carpets, they are kept postcard perfect by chemical fertilizers, herbicides, riding lawnmowers and leaf-blowers. With each rainfall, these chemicals flow freely into adjacent bayous and wetlands, eventually finding their way to the ocean. These nitrogen-rich fertilizers starve the water of oxygen, threatening marine life and human activity alike, amplifying red-tide algal blooms and the poisonous brevetoxins they produce. They are not only deadly to marine life, but also dangerous to people who inadvertently breathe in tiny droplets of ocean spray that can be full of the deadly toxins. Red tides, carried by wind and waves, shut down beaches if they come ashore; they close oyster and shrimp harvesting sites and ban commercial and sport fishing. Fish killed by red tides can wash ashore to decay in the hot sun, further exacerbating an already unhealthy problem, while wrecking communities dependent on ocean goers. The livelihood of shrimpers and oyster farmers,

Students examine a juvenile shark washed up on the shore near Bolivar Flats, the thin span of ocean that separates Galveston Bay from the Gulf of Mexico and used by ocean-going vessels to enter Port Houston.

mom-and-pop businesses catering to sport fishers, and the many other small businesses that count on ocean recreation in general can be ruined.

Red tide is only one symptom of an unhealthy coastal environment. The larger impacts brought about by unmanaged development, poor long-term use of estuaries, shrinking natural habitats, and general neglect seem to have no end in sight. Compromised ecological systems are the result of profit-based temperament, laissez-faire governmental control, and the ecological illiteracy of the almost-seven-million people living in the counties bordering the Texas Gulf Coast.

Red tide, red necks, and unchecked development are not peculiar to Texas or even to the Gulf. Around the world, coastal edges increasingly draw new industry, residents, and visitors. Fragile coastal environments comprise only about ten percent of the earth's surface, yet these thin strips of habitable land are home to over 3.7 billion people. Coastal cities are among the fastest growing in the world; eleven of the world's sixteen megacities are situated on the ocean: Shanghai, Los Angeles, Mumbai, Manila, Kolkata, and New York, to name a few. Though their circumstances differ, all are threatened by rising sea levels. Some are more prepared than others. Just look at lower Manhattan after Hurricane Sandy and the devastation there. What will happen fifty years from now when sea levels may be one foot higher in New York harbor? Plans are in place to fortify Lower Manhattan's Bay edge, yet as in Texas, it's a slippery slope, likely to have unintended ecological consequences that can't yet be imagined. Places like the Mekong River Delta and the Ganges River basin, some of the most densely populated—and poorest—on the planet, will be impacted the most. The world over, regions like these face a grim forfeiture of human life, not to mention their cultural richness

This worldwide ecological emergency shapes the work and thinking of the Gulf Coast DesignLab in fundamental ways. As humanity's existential crisis rapidly unfolds, among the current generation of students I see an ever-growing acceptance that they are about to be the first generation fully caught in climate disaster's death grip. These designers of tomorrow are acutely aware that their lives are about to fundamentally change. Most feel they'll have less a secure future life than the one they now have. As a consequence, many of their older generation—people my age—are asking ourselves whether what we're teaching them today will be relevant when they're forty, sixty, or eighty years old. Will they look back on the early-twenty-first century as that tragically-missed moment, when instead of committing to deep societal change, their futures were traded for short-term self-interest and lack of collective imagination? Will they wonder why their educational institutions—and those of us who taught them—so thoroughly failed in preparing them for difficult times ahead? More and more, students in design school question the very need for the profession of architecture in the way it exists today, serving only the very few who can afford our services. They wonder if they are on a path that will matter, when so much is at stake. Moreover, why be committed to much of anything when the very existence of humanity could be in the balance? The question of whether we are preparing them for a future—that will much different than our present—is threefold: are we giving our students the skills and tools they will need, are we instilling in them a sense of much-needed urgency, and are we inspiring them to muster the heart and soul needed to cope with the unfolding crisis. These are hard, ethical questions on which we educators, for the most part, seem to be mute.

Student from BRIDGE research the Valero petroleum plant that borders a public park in Houston's fenceline community, the Harrisburg neighborhood. © Coleman Coker

Students from DUNE document a large ocean-going vessel entering Corpus Christi Bay from the Gulf.

A student from RISE sketches wetlands grasses along the boardwalk near the Intracoastal Waterway.

Today's students are not the first to question their future, though. In 1995, the celebrated cosmologist Dr. Carl Sagan and the respected evolutionary biologist Dr. Ernst Mayr famously argued the probability of intelligent life elsewhere in the cosmos.[1] Sagan described the universe as filled with innumerable planets just like earth and posited that some of them must undoubtedly harbor life, just as intelligent and as curious as we are. Mayr took the position that it is very unlikely this is the case. He pointed out that his argument was validated by our very own earth and its evolutionary history, of which we are a part. He agreed that there is indeed intelligence on earth, but intelligence of this kind—which we humans possess—is a sort of lethal mutation, and will not be long-lived. He supported his position by examining the success of biological entities as a whole—measuring their success by how many lifeforms of that particular species existed. The most successful species succeed because they rapidly mutate to take over large and otherwise diverse areas—he used bacteria as an example—which become fine-tuned to their environments. Evolution fit them into very specific ecological niches where they stabilized and have survived successfully for millions of years—beetles are a good example—because of their interdependent relationship with the environment.

However, mammals, compared to organisms like insects, are very few. And the highest order of mammals, we humans, who have been around for only a short time on the geological clock scale, are even fewer in number and not adjusted to our environment. From a contemporary perspective, we appear to have overpopulated the earth causing ecological catastrophe; however, as Mayr demonstrated, this has only been the case for the last couple-hundred years—just a tick on the geologic clock. Spread out over our hundred-thousand-year existence, there have been relatively few of us. Mayr also pointed out that the lifespan of the existence of higher intelligent mammals seems to be about one-hundred-thousand years, roughly the time humans have been on earth. His deduction is that it's highly unlikely to find intelligent life on other planets—or here on earth over time—because highly intelligent species historically only have very short existences, often due to ecological imbalance. As the scale of intelligence in organisms increases, historically there is less and less long-term success—neither bacteria nor beetles are giants of intelligence; and even bacteria, with its rapid reproductive growth, if not kept in check, eventually kills its host. And unlike effectively adaptive beetles, we humans have done a very poor job at becoming environmentally interdependent. Consequently, higher intelligence like ours is, according to Mayr, an unnatural outcome. It is a mutation, and mutations don't live long. They eventually destroy their host and consequently themselves, thus dying out altogether.

We seem to be on the road of fulfilling Dr. Mayr's prognostication. In my lifetime, the world's population has more than tripled, from two-and-one-half-billion to now eight-billion, and that number is still rising. Crowding most every corner of the earth, these many billions have so undermined the planet's ecological vitality that half the number of the wildlife that existed just fifty years ago has now disappeared. We have so altered the face of the earth that over half its fertile land is now utilized for monoculture crops and our bovine friends. Speaking of them, if the world's cattle were measured by the amount of CO_2 they produce, they would be the third-largest country on the planet, behind the United States and China. If humans and the domestic animals we raise were counted together, we'd amount to ninety-six percent of animal mass on earth, the other four-percent being what's left of "wild" creatures. One third of wild fish species have been over-fished to the point of collapse. Rising oceans are causing land to disappear at rates not seen in hundreds of thousands of years. Rivers are running dry. Consider the massive extinction of whole species occurring at such an alarming rate that we have coined a name for it: the "Sixth Extinction."[2]

What is happening is perhaps best summed up by E. O. Wilson, "The one process now going on that will take millions of years to correct is the loss of

As a way to familiarize themselves with the ecology of Galveston Bay where they'll be working, students from SHIFT help plant wetland grasses, as a means to establish a healthier bay system. © Coleman Coker

genetic and species diversity by the destruction of natural habitats. This is the folly our descendants are least likely to forgive us."[3]

Closer to home, where Gulf Coast DesignLab students work, viable aquatic habitats, coastal wetlands, and sheltering bay waters have disappeared at alarming rates. Their destruction is particularly devastating since these aquatic nurseries are some of the richest life-giving biomes on the planet. Including the billions of tons of CO_2 being spewed from petrochemical smokestacks and automobile tailpipes here in Texas and around the world, unchecked drilling for petroleum and natural gas flares combine to pump inordinate amounts of methane into the air. The damming and spoiling of rivers emptying into the Gulf have cut off fertile bayou and wetland nutrients necessary for ocean life. Some years, the Rio Grande is bone-dry by the time it reaches the Gulf. Far to the north, warming oceans have reduced artic ice over forty percent in the last fifty years. Icecaps are disappearing so rapidly it is predicted that in less than twenty-five years there will no longer be an arctic ice cap in the summer months. Greenland ice is now disappearing at such a rapid annual rate that some scientists now say it has already reached its tipping point and is not likely to recover for centuries. Further south, skies in the western United States are seasonally turning an eerie Bladerunner-orange, the result of the dense shroud of smoke from incinerating forests. The same is happening in northern Canada, Russia, and Alaska. Add to this the deforestation of equatorial rainforests and circumpolar boreal wildernesses. Climate norms have gone haywire.

"My undergrad degree was in environmental studies so I very much understood climate change. The hands-on work we did in studio really cemented that this was a serious issue."

— Nieve Tierney, RISE

This mass undoing is because of our technological acumen, which has given us free reign to use up the planet as we see fit. In less than one-hundred years we've extracted fossil fuels that took millions of years to transform from once-living matter. We've turned that ancient matter into petroleum and plastics, consuming it in a seemingly endless now-you-see-it-now-you-don't kind of magic. All this for short-term convenience and seemingly bottomless consumerism. We humans are indeed a mighty and destructive force, altering the earth in ways that just a few hundred years ago would have been unimaginable. Even if we stopped emitting hydrocarbons today, temperatures around the world will continue to rise, bringing greater fire risk, crop failure, death, and increased poverty. Oceans will continue to warm, melting more polar ice, causing sea levels to rise, forcing whole populations into becoming climate migrants. The level of disruption scientists recently believed was twenty years off is happening now, and we see unpredictable acceleration with each passing year. The now-unfolding feedback loops will continue for centuries. By many accounts, we've passed a tipping point that's sure to usher in a slow-moving catastrophe. Every year goes by with less chance of holding it back. This is not alarmist doomsaying; this is well-established facts backed by credible science.

What then, is our future? Are humans indeed on the way out? If it is permissible to turn to science fiction for a moment, in the 1999 film, The Matrix, Agent Smith "share(s) a revelation" with Morpheus, telling him that we humans are "...a virus. Human beings are a disease, a cancer on this planet, (we) are a plague." In Matrix-world, a higher level of intelligence was needed to keep human passions in check, to prevent us from destroying the planet and, in turn, ourselves. Is Agent Smith correct? Are we in fact an invasive parasite locked in an ever-combative guest-host relationship with the earth, one that, like the virus, eventually kills its host and destroys itself in the process? Or, is this scenario just an imaginary sci-fi story dreamed up by the Wachowski sisters—a fantasy narrative that coincidentally aligns with Dr. Mayr's diagnosis? Are we—in the harm we're bringing to the earth—a plague? As Mayr describes, is it because of our higher intelligence, which brought about our technological advancements—a technology that has now escaped our ability to control because of a powerlessness to curb our wants? Are we really an abnormality because we've evolved to "think"? The technological cunning of this species of bipeds that in geologic terms has been around for only the blink of an eye is the cause of planetary-changing events.

"Weeks before we began designing, we studied environmental issues facing the Gulf Coast and the relationship between climate change and the petrochemical industry there and ways to address it and help mitigate the toll taken on communities and the environment."
— **Christie Johnson, BRIDGE**

But there is another way of looking at this catastrophe, one that doesn't seem as unnatural. It challenges Dr. Myer's and Agent Smith's framing of humans as a mutating virus. It grew out of the early days of the environmental movement where humans were considered an evolutionary manifestation of the earth itself, not as unnatural or separate from it, not even as particularly special. We're not intelligent beings living on this planet; we are this planet, an expression of earth's ongoing evolutionary process, the latest actant refashioning this earth to bring about rapid and massive change. As an evolutionary manifestation of a changing Earth, could we be compared to the Chicxulub meteor that killed most life on earth, ushering in a new era of biological beings? Or could our treatment of the planet yield similar self-destruction as that of early anaerobic life, which killed itself off with its own poisonous oxygen waste? Could we be earth's mechanism similar to earlier super volcanic eruptions that spewed toxic gases into the atmosphere, blocking out the sun and killing off most of life? Scientific evidence tells us there have been five planet-wide extinctions, and we are bringing about the sixth. It begs the question of whether we are no more than the latest dynamic agent that sways the planet's ever-moving pendulum, causing the latest cycle of emergence where the old makes way for the new. Is it so hard to imagine ourselves as earth's latest evolutionary agent of system-wide change? In this light, whether our intellect is a mutation or not misses the point. Our technological acumen, and the way we have used it, is merely earth's latest ongoing change maker. This may seem radical to some, written off as a psilocybin-induced fantasy of vexing environmentalists who just stumbled onto

Using heavy equipment borrowed from the McFaddin National Wildlife Refuge, workers prepare to relocate the surprisingly intact FLOAT, which was carried almost a mile inland by Hurricane Harvey. © Coleman Coker

extraordinary mushrooms. But set aside the flesh, bones, consciousness, and soul for a moment and think of humans as an enormous system of energy—a worldwide, interrelated verb instead of a bunch of disconnected nouns. Perhaps we're not unlike the wind and waves that cause barrier islands to change, re-form, and change again. We change the earth, reshape it, move it about, make it something different: we, the engine of ever-shifting dynamic equilibrium.

One thing Mayr and Agent Smith didn't take into account, though, is that our level of intelligence, mutation or not, gives us the ability to make choices. We have the capacity to choose which paths we take. On a global scale—where we're interconnected by one of the outcomes of the very technology that can destroy us—we can decide to cooperatively change course and bypass the path that leads to our own demise. Together, we can, through profound and rapid change, take the path of discovery and seek another version of ourselves in a way that would fundamentally change our relationship to the world. We see this beginning to unfold, with what's happening right here at home. While the thirty million residents of Texas would make it the fiftieth largest nation on the planet—if Texas were its own country—it's disproportionally the world's seventh largest emitter of greenhouse gases. Yet, Texas is now the largest wind power producer in the United States and ranks only second to California in solar energy production. And more solar and wind farms are being built here every year. There are the recently announced wind farms off the Galveston and Port Arthur coast—the first in the Gulf of Mexico—that together will cover almost half-a-million acres and power over two million homes. Houston is one of a handful of American cities that's on track to meet its Paris agreement target of carbon output production by 2050. The city is about to become home to the largest urban solar farm in the country, sited on an abandoned landfill that will not only power five-thousand homes but help revitalize one of the city's most economically-depressed neighborhoods, with a number of the farm's new jobs set aside for local residents. Close to Dallas, AT&T, Honda, McDonalds, Google, The Home Depot and several small Texas towns recently came together to help build what will be the nation's largest solar farm, producing enough electricity to power over three-hundred thousand homes. Not just in the Lone Star state, everywhere we turn, we see our relationship to the world transforming. Stories like these are becoming commonplace. Motivating us to even more effectual action, they offer the capacity to reimagine ourselves as a different measure of earth's evolution, one that mirrors and even magnifies the interrelatedness of life on earth. It is up to us to commit to that path. It is a choice we must make.

We are be able to transform our present course if we're willing to rally collective narratives of change and to act on them with conviction. This potential is as old as the communal stories told around ancient campfires. It is a characteristic of ours that Dr. Mayr and Agent Smith didn't factor into their equation; these are the stories we tell ourselves that shape us into who we can be.

So often, we have created new narratives at just the right historical moment, stories that comfortably fit the need at hand, stories that have transformed who we are to who we can be. The narrative that shapes now—fashioned around desire, an overabundance of unnecessary things, a sense of individualism at the expense of community, not looking after those who are less fortunate than us, imagining we're somehow apart from the earth that keeps us alive—need to change. We are on a path of destroying the earth, of sacrificing the world's poorest for our own Western-style comfort, of caring about ourselves while forgetting our neighbors' needs. Each day the news provides us with fresh stories of doom and gloom. But must we tacitly accept this narrative leading us astray? We have a choice in how we respond to what is happening. We have the ability to craft a fresh narrative that provides a renewed sense of who we are, of who we might become. We have the collective compassion to set aside selfish interests and work together to achieve the unachievable, to make lasting change that benefits all, not for just the few who hide away in fortified strongholds. If we give in to the rampant nihilism that infects so much of contemporary society, then we have little incentive to push back against what are otherwise insurmountable odds. If we hope to overcome despair and act with wisdom, we can ethically rethink our relationship with the earth and with each other. We can start shaping this collective narrative that works toward the common good of all. It is the much-needed antidote to the pessimism that now shapes many of our lives.

"I consider myself to be relatively well-informed about how dire the climate crisis is, yet the GCDL helped me begin to pay more attention, particularly to fenceline communities in the shadows of chemical refineries that suffer deadly consequences."
— Laura Marley Lancaster, BRIDGE

This new story sets aside our hubris and the dead-end path we are on now, telling us that not every problem we face has a technological solution. It is a tale that says the annual GNP is not a true way to value collective achievement, compelling us to value what worth really means: well-being for all, care for one another, our health and the planet's protection, a robust environment that makes room for every species to thrive. The story we tell can remind us how to accept the value of others, that we're no more important than the mockingbird on the telephone pole outside the window, the Yellowstone wolf that just had her first litter of pups, the poorest child in southeast Asia, or the financially oppressed people in every corner of the world. The narrative can include how our insistent control of all that is about us harms us, how we learned to become better listeners to each other and to the desires of this earth. It can encourage a new kind of animism that merges with scientific veracity, making us better witnesses to the marvels of this universe. It is discovering beauty in the most common weed growing in our vegetable garden. It can teach us to respect what we do not know instead of relying on quick-solution-based answers before we fully understand their long-term implications. It can teach us that there is mystery all around us that we will never master. We can learn how the things we make are beautiful, not because we deem them aesthetically pleasing but because they were made with the interrelated whole of the earth in mind. And it can teach us that we are the earth and the earth is us—that when we do harm to it, we harm ourselves. It is a story of compassion, a tale of love and commitment. In our own tiny way, the work we do at the Gulf Coast DesignLab is a hopeful response to this desire for change. We are one little comma in the great narrative of change that needs to happen if our students—and the generations to follow—are to shed their tacit acceptance of a lesser life ahead and desire living in a more equitable, thriving world. We all can play a small part in shaping this new story. If you want to make sure that Dr. Mayr and Agent Smith are dead wrong, it's time to roll up your sleeves and get to work!

Endnotes

1 Noam Chomsky, "Human Intelligence and the Environment," Lecture, University of North Carolina, Chapel Hill, 30 September 2010. https://chomsky.info/20100930/

2 Elizabeth Kolbert, *The Sixth Extinction, An Unnatural History*, (New York: Picador, Henry Holt and Company, 2015).

3 E. O. Wilson, *Biophilia*, (Cambridge, Massachusetts and London, England: Harvard University Press, 1984) 121.

All indented quotes from GCDL alumni and clients are drawn from questionaire responses or interviews with Sarah Gamble.

A student helps repair the damaged roof of a small home on Lamar Peninsula torn away during Hurricane Harvey.
© Coleman Coker

Students test out their just completed project IGNITE, a new fire circle gathering area and monarch butterfly waystation for the San Jacinto Girl Scouts' new property on Galveston Island.
© Coleman Coker

The fire from GATHER reflects off oyster shells in the gabion wall.
© Luke Stevenson

GATHER
FLOAT
RISE
STORE
INHABIT
OBSERVE
SHIFT
COOP

GATHER

FALL 2014

Location: Goose Island State Park
Client: Texas Parks & Wildlife Department
Design Team: Director: Coleman Coker; Students: Rachel Duggan, Katherine Eastman, Jamie Epley, Huiming Zuo (Zoe), Thomas Johnston, Kuan Liu, Celine Pinto, Ruihua Cai (Mark), Luke Stevenson, Teng Li (James)
Awards: 2015 American Society of Landscape Architects (ASLA) national Student Collaboration Award; 2014-2015 University of Texas at Austin School of Architecture Design Excellence Award

Sometimes, a successful collaboration between a client and a designer becomes the spark for something more. GATHER, a fire circle at Goose Island State Park, is the first of three projects within the park and five total GCDL projects with committed partner and state agency, Texas Parks & Wildlife Department (TPWD). Goose Island is located eight miles north of Fulton, Texas, and sits on the edge of the St. Charles Bay, where the Copano and Aransas bays converge. The park is abundant with educational opportunities, including plant identification, stargazing, and learning about the importance of reestablishing oyster reefs, but it is best known for the large population of migratory birds that stop over in the park to refuel on their way south. Dense live oaks with thick underbrush blanket the landscape, including the thousand-year-old "Big Tree" that is one of the nation's largest live oaks. One of the top ten most visited state parks in Texas, Goose Island is popular with youth, drawing scout troops and others most weekends and for longer periods over the summer. To further support youth camping in the park, TPWD partnered with GCDL to design and construct a fire circle to serve as a new gathering point for educational programming and informal activities.

In the Fall 2014 semester, TPWD embarked upon their first project with the Gulf Coast DesignLab, creating a symbiotic collaboration with environmental education at its core. TPWD challenged students to design and build a new piece of social infrastructure for the Goose Island State Park's Youth Area. The existing area was a large sandy clearing within the thick live oak, providing half an acre of open space for tent camping and gathering for a typically sized scout troop. The existing tree line shaped the expansive outdoor room and provided a visual barrier from the nearby recreational vehicle camping area. TPWD requested the circle provide seating for twenty individuals to serve the visiting youth and become the starting point for their popular walking tours through the dense live oak in that part of the park and stargazing activities lead by the park's nature interpreter.

Guests to Goose Island State Park enjoy the warmth of the winter sun while seated around the fire pit of GATHER.
© Henry Yamamoto

GCDL students began the design process by exploring the landscape and learning about local materials. The park's nature interpreter, Janelle Rand, asked the students to study shellcrete structures in the area and try to incorporate the material into their design. She explained how the material could be used as a tool for educational presentations and foster discussion about water-cleansing oysters and their role in the bay's ecosystem. Students visited El Copano, an abandoned seaport town on Copano Bay once used by pirates and smugglers and later by the Spanish to support incoming immigrants and early mission sites farther inland. In the 18th and 19th centuries, because of the lack of wood to build with, the port community utilized shellcrete, a durable material that took advantage of the abundance of oyster shells on the coast. (The dense live oaks seen in the park today are primarily the result of later European settlers.) Oysters shells were burned over an open fire for several days, reducing them to calcium oxide, also known as quicklime. When combined with whole oyster shells, sand, and water, the mixture has properties similar to concrete and is well suited to the coastal climate. Having studied the shellcrete firsthand, the students set out to incorporate the material into their design for its longevity and teaching opportunities. Through trial and error, they made more than thirty test blocks, each one-foot-by-one-foot, to hone in on the correct proportions until they found the right mix.

Within the clearing on the site, students oriented the project to face the east, placing a seven-foot-high gabion wall to the west to block views of the adjacent parking area and strong western sun in the late afternoon. The gabions work with the existing tree line to create a sense of enclosure—essentially an outdoor

GATHER students document the tiny marine life thriving off of the recently washed up sargassum.
© Henry Yamamoto

GATHER students boat across Copano Bay to visit early 19th-century structures built of "shellcrete," a low-tech building material to make settlement homes. Shellcrete was developed by European colonists, using the abundant oyster shells found in Texas bays.
© Henry Yamamoto

GATHER students document deteriorating shellcrete structures, a calcium carbonate-based concrete. Oyster shells are heated over a fire until they become a fine power. Crushed shells and beach sand are used as aggregate. When mixed in the right proportions with water, the concrete can be shaped into walls that last a century or more.
© Henry Yamamoto

room-within-a-room. The gabions are composed of vertical steel I-beams with hog wire mesh holding 120 cubic feet of oyster shells. To compliment the vertical element, students created a series of concrete and shellcrete volumes to anchor the steel firepit and support surrounding seating platforms. Shellcrete also composes the inner circle and firepit, with a more traditional Portland cement concrete mix forming the seating area's outer edges and the base of extended stargazing platform on the southern side. Students sandblasted the shellcrete to reveal the oyster shell aggregate within and accentuate its light color in contrast to the darker grays of Portland cement concrete mixtures. Resting on top of the shellcrete and concrete volumes, with a three-quarter inch separation to prevent rot, horizontal wood panels composed of sandwiched two-by-four treated pine with one-inch thick oak spacers provide more tactile seating for visitors.

Tj Hinojosa, assistant superintendent at Goose Island, reports that since GATHER's completion in December 2014, its use has been "constant" and aligned with its original intent. The youth area, anchored by GATHER and CANOPY (a covered eating space completed by GCDL in 2015), often provides a "home base" for visiting groups camping in the area or for larger groups that may be camping throughout the park. Hinojosa commended the overall durability of the project yet reported challenges with the loose oyster shells, which visitors are pulling from the vertical gabions and moving to unintended places within the park. He pointed to the probability the material won't be used in this way in the future. Despite the issue, Hinojosa reflects on the unique experience created by the local material: "In the evenings, I patrol the park—and when there's a fire at that pit in the youth area, there is this really cool orange and yellowish curtain that comes through the shells, because there's a fire behind it. You can see the light peek through all the shells—it's a cool experience to see and it's a different way of seeing a fire."[1]

— Sarah Gamble

Endnotes

1 Tj Hinojosa (Texas Parks & Wildlife) in discussion with the author, 22 November 2021.

Returning from their first field trip, GATHER students begin sharing initial design ideas with their classmates.
© Coleman Coker.

The park's nature interpreter uses the fire pit seating of GATHER to show images that describe indigenous plant life common to the Gulf Coast area, of which Goose Island is a part.

A view of GATHER from the entry side. The park's nature interpreter places a telescope on the wood deck for visitor star gazing nights.
© Coleman Coker

GATHER students celebrate the completion of their project by testing the fire pit to enjoy its warmth and glow.
© Luke Stevenson

FLOAT at sunrise
reflecting off
the wetland waters.
© Evan Greulich

FLOAT

SPRING 2016

Location: Sea Rim State Park
Client: Texas Parks & Wildlife Department
Design Team: Director: Coleman Coker; Students: Nevin Blum,Michelle Cantu, Connie Chang, Claire Fontaine, Evan Greulich, Asher Intebi, Marissa Jordan, Estrella Juarez, Kelsey Kaiser, Kevin Keating, Amy McDonald, Ashley Nguyen, Raquel Royal
Awards: 2017 Texas Society of Architects Design Award

FLOAT, a first-of-its-kind camping platform for Texas Parks & Wildlife Department (TPWD), was constructed over four days of work by Gulf Coast DesignLab students, who assembled ten prefabricated modules in the wetland site. Nestled on the northernmost edge of the Texas Gulf Coast, Sea Rim State Park is a fragile, yet harsh landscape with 4,000 acres of wetlands along 5.2 miles of coastline. The area, located near the many petrochemical plants in Port Arthur, has seen a surge of development and pollution, loss of native habitat, and repeat damage from natural disasters. Hurricane Rita hit the park hard in 2005, then Ike came ashore in 2008, destroying park infrastructure twice within three years. When it came time to rebuild, TPWD called upon the Gulf Coast DesignLab to create a new, resilient amenity within the aquatic landscape.

The idea to design and build a platform campsite in the Spring 2016 semester developed from an initial conversation between GCDL director Coleman Coker and Sea Rim State Park Superintendent Nathan Londenberg, who wanted to make the wetlands more accessible and draw visitors into the vastly underutilized area of the park. The floating campsite idea was unique, as it would become one of few "backcountry" camping opportunities within the state park system, which is dominated by drive-up "car camping" sites. While FLOAT welcomes the public, the project was particularly attractive to GCDL because of the scientists, bird counters, and biologists who could also utilize the platform for their investigations. The superintendent's original program called for two campsites, one sized for four guests and one for two guests, to be designed in keeping with the park's "leave no trace" policy, which required careful consideration of camping trash and restroom needs for overnight visitors.

Throughout the design process, students carefully considered how they would assemble the project within four feet of water over a few short days. To meet the extreme construction challenges, students would need to design and fabricate the structure on-campus in a componentized way; each piece could be no more than four feet wide for transport by flat-bottom boat in shallow water of the winding bayou leading to the environmentally sensitive site. Students also

Returning from their first field trip and visit to the project's site, students begin their design work for FLOAT.
© Coleman Coker

While preparing for their design work, students get an orientation from Sea Rim State Park's superintendent.
© Coleman Coker

Students camp on the beach in Sea Rim State Park as they prepare for tomorrow's first visit to the FLOAT work site.

FLOAT students familiarize themselves with the local ecology by kayaking the area around their future work site.
© Coleman Coker

FLOAT's "mast" acts a way-finding device for kayakers moving through tall wetland grasses of Sea Rim State Park.
© Kelsey Kaiser

needed to be cognizant of the native alligator population when planning their onsite assembly and future use of the campsite; they even conferred with an alligator expert to guide their decision-making. Following a final design review and budget assessment, TPWD and the GCDL team collaboratively decided to prioritize the larger four-person campsite and eliminate the two-person campsite from the project.

With less than $10,000 for materials and associated costs, the thirteen-student design team created a functional outpost and captivating marker within the delicate environment. Students fabricated multiple components on the UT Austin campus for transport by trailer to the state park and then by flat-bottom boat for a four-day weekend assembly on the water. With limited workspace, students took shifts assembling the prefabricated parts of the floating platform first, while the remaining students kept watch in kayaks for alligators. Once assembled, the platform—composed of eight floats and four weights to hold the campsite in place—then provided a working surface for on-site welding and assembly of the remaining pieces.

Visitors spot the tower, which acts as a wayfinding device, thirty minutes into a sixty-minute paddle from the dock to the campsite. The tower is wrapped in a semi-open wood screen of vertical members that accentuates its verticality, while creating an interior of sorts. The students were deliberate in their shaping of a vertical form that might reference the oil rigs not far from the park's coastal shore in distant Port Arthur, generating questions about the region's environmental health and industrial players. The tower also provides privacy to visitors using the campsite's basic toilet, which requires a conventional five-gallon bucket that visitors bring back to shore for emptying. Exposed steel rails, recessed within the platform's surface, allow for tents to be easily tied down in wind. Raised horizontal rails around the platform's perimeter keep alligators from climbing onto the platform surface and act as a delicate register against the water. Through its materiality and form, FLOAT successfully draws out the inherent contrasts of place as a dynamic gesture within the protected landscape.

Since FLOAT's completion in May 2016, the public can experience the beauty and uncommon quiet of this wetland wilderness atop the platform. Campsite reservations can be made through TPWD on a first-come, first-served basis. In Fall 2016, two adjustments were made to the project: a customized "crown" was added to the tower to combat its use as a cormorant perch and the increasing volume of avian excrement; and welded steel components were added to each of the four concrete anchors to increase the project's weight and resistance to movement caused by strong winds. In Fall 2017, FLOAT went offline for four weeks following Hurricane Harvey. The campsite was pushed nearly one-half mile from its site into the adjacent preserve, yet it escaped damage. FLOAT was returned to service with help from preserve staff and heavy machinery borrowed from nearby McFaddin National Wildlife Refuge. The back-country campsite has continued to see steady use, averaging forty reservations per year, largely one- to two-night weekend stays, with an uptick to over fifty reservations in 2021.[1] FLOAT has garnered praise from users as well as designers, including the 2017 Texas Society of Architects Design Awards Jury, which praised the design for its simplicity and multi-dimensionality despite the technical challenges of the site. The jury noted the project's successes in tectonics and detailing, highlighting the integration of wood and steel. The project was honored with one of eleven awards that year for its design excellence and impact, selected out of 313 project entries.[2] As jury member David Miller explains, "The tower becomes this amazing landmark and beautiful signpost, a counterpoint to the strong horizon of the waterway."[3]

— Sarah Gamble

Acknowledgments

A previous version of this project description was first published as "FLOAT" in *Texas Architect*, as part of its 2017 Design Awards issue.

Endnotes

1 Texas Parks & Wildlife Department, Reservation data provided to the author, July 22, 2019 and Nov 16, 2021.
2 Alyssa Morris, "2017 Design Award Winners", *Texas Architect* (blog news), 17 May 2017. https://magazine.texasarchitects.org/2017/05/17/2017-design-award-winners/.
3 *Texas Architect*, Notes from Jury Deliberations for Texas Society of Architects 2017 Design Awards, provided to the author, April 2017.

Just a small fraction of the many iterations sketched during FLOAT's design process.
© Evan Greulich, 3

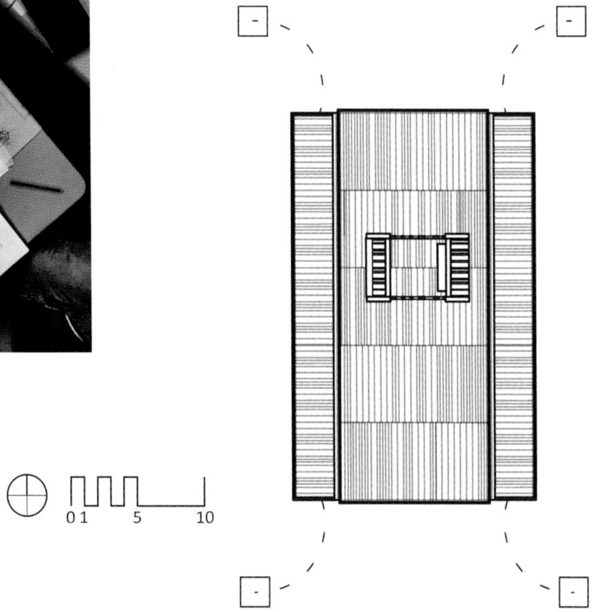

Using the courtyard area of the school, students test their design ideas at full scale, determining the appropriate size of FLOAT's deck.
© Coleman Coker

Students kayak forty-five minutes to their work site, followed by another forty-five-minute trip back after a long day's work on FLOAT.
© Amy McDonald

To minimize construction time on the water, deck panels for FLOAT were prefabricated on campus and snapped into place on the floating frame. The entire project was put together and finished in five days.
© Coleman Coker

Up to their waists in water, students install components to help complete FLOAT.
© Amy McDonald

A student welds the four prefabricated sides of the mast together in preparation for raising it.
© Coleman Coker

A group effort is needed to lift the mast of FLOAT into place.
© Kelsey Kaiser

Once the project is completed FLOAT is moved to its final resting place where students dropped concrete anchors.
© Amy McDonald

A toilet seat built within the mast's volume accommodates a five-gallon bucket to transport waste back to shore. Note the crescent moon over the doorway, a reference to outhouses once in the rural South.
© Asher Intebi

FLOAT students incorporated flush steel rails into the deck for securing tents.
© Coleman Coker

Visitors arrive to FLOAT by kayak, bringing all the provisions needed for a weekend stay.
© Coleman Coker

FLOAT's mast is opaque at the base, where privacy is needed for the toilet within, and porous at the top to accommodate breezes and keep it from over-turning during high winds and hurricanes.
© Coleman Coker

Sunset over the Gulf.
© Coleman Coker

A first step for students working in the Galveston Bay area is research on the many petrochemical facilities that dominate the Galveston Bay coastline, known as the "energy coast."
© Coleman Coker

CHAPTER 2

Gulf Coast DesignLab: A Model for Learning

Sarah Gamble

"Once we begin to know our environment, we will want to nurture and protect it," explains Coleman Coker, architect, educator, and director of the Gulf Coast DesignLab. Following his time in post-Katrina New Orleans, Coker has spent the past decade engaging in teaching from an ecologically focused perspective. "I realized that if environmental education had been a priority over previous decades, the outcome of Hurricane Katrina would have been very different."[1] Reflecting on his Baby Boomer generation and their approach to architectural practice, Coker could no longer ignore the pressing environmental crisis and teach architectural studios in the ways he had in the past, which focused more on form and aesthetics. He set out to develop a new program that would shape the next generation of designers with a deep respect for the natural environment, while working to assist environmental educators in their efforts to engage the public.[2]

Established in 2012 at the University of Texas at Austin School of Architecture, the Gulf Coast DesignLab immerses students in the Texas Gulf Coast, an area of great beauty under tremendous pressure from frequent hurricanes, wetland degradation, and new development. The dynamic coastline challenges students to rethink how they get to know and respond to a project's context, while the collaborative studio offers hands-on lessons and experience in designing for a specific place and its people. Each semester, students work with a nonprofit or public agency to design and build a small structure or educational tool that supports local environmental education efforts for K-12 students, individuals with disabilities, and the general public. Addressing clients' specific needs, GCDL students create spaces for ecologists, biologists, and naturalists to teach and research, and for the public to learn and experience the Gulf Coast firsthand. Their projects are completed in collaboration with nonprofit and governmental stakeholder clients, each with a focus on environmental education. Clients own the project sites and provide all of the funding for these design-build projects, ranging from $7,000 to $35,000 per built structure. The construction funds are matched by students' time, tools owned by GCDL, and travel support from the School of Architecture. Between 2012 and 2022, GCDL has completed twenty-nine projects, including twenty-seven built structures (twenty-sixcurrently in use and one destroyed by Hurricane Harvey) and two hands-on educational tools for classroom use, with participation from more than 350 architecture, interiors, and landscape architecture students at the undergraduate and graduate levels.

A pioneering ecologically based architecture studio, the Gulf Coast DesignLab fosters environmental education not just for the students who participate, but also for the public its projects serve. Innovative yet straightforward, the GCDL process provides a strong model for architectural education and practice in the Anthropocene. To further ideas proposed by the GCDL and encourage the application of the model elsewhere, the bulk of this chapter focuses on careful documentation and analysis of the program in seven sections: Optimism and Design-Build Pedagogy, Engagement with Site and Client, Project Origins and Programmatic Needs, Collaboration in Design, Material Specificity, Balancing Time and Budget, and Leadership and Teaching. These topics pose expansive, yet fundamental questions for the profession and demonstrate the exponential impact small projects can have in response to large social and environmental problems.

GCDL students plant native coastal prairie grasses with local middle-school students from area schools.

Students from BLIND SIDED listen to their classmate play a trumpet dirge for a dead whale recently washed ashore on Mustang Island and subsequently buried beneath the sand dune on which they are resting.
© Coleman Coker

Optimism and design-build pedagogy

"Design-build pedagogy embraces the fullness of architecture as an optimistic act. For architecture extends an offering to the world each time a design is built," writes educator and design-build practitioner Adam Hopfner in his foreword to *The Design-Build Studio: Crafting Meaningful Work in Architectural Education.*[3] A spirit of optimism is central to the Gulf Coast DesignLab. Students learn about the beauty and fragility of the natural environment, while bolstering confidence in their ability to tackle the environmental crisis through their work. While most would classify GCDL as "design-build," a project delivery model that challenges students to realize a design through construction, Coker shies away from labeling the work in this way. To him, the design-build process is his vehicle of choice to integrate lessons of environmental education, justice, and activism into the design studio—and he prefers highlighting these topics instead (primary example: the title of this book). Consistent with many programs in which students design and construct work across the United States, GCDL collaborates with clients and communities as they work to meet a specific need through tangible means. GCDL takes the concept a step further by tailoring the selection of clients and projects to those with a focus on environmental education, ensuring the clients benefit from the construction of spaces that enable them to expand their teaching capacity and mission, while the design students develop their environmental literacy throughout the realizing of a design for the client.

As they grapple with larger questions about the profession and how they will practice in the future, GCDL students engage in the tangible realities of material and assembly—an experience that can be inherently transformative to a young designer. They get a glimpse of professional practice and the construction process, asking questions and making decisions about essential facets of practice not often covered in a design (only) studio. As is common with most design-build programs, limited budgets, academic semester schedules, and the proficiency of students dictate a maximum size and level of complexity for these student projects, yet these limitations also present valuable lessons and benefits to the process. Without interiors or conditioned spaces to contend with, students can't lean on sustainability add-ons or integrated technologies that may lead to quick fixes. The students are challenged to address architecture at its most basic, structure and skin, as they are guided by the environment.

While the program has won numerous awards for its excellence in design, Coker believes GCDL's success is tied to its nested approach to learning: integrating lessons of civic responsibility, collaboration, and environmental education within a design-build studio format. This approach is a shift from many architectural studio agendas, which place design at the top of a hierarchical list of goals and objectives. For Coker, "the architectural product becomes a residue of the process ... The process is trying to get students to grow—and be wed to the condition they are working with. Architecture becomes the vehicle for environmental education."[4]

While good design remains a tacitly central concern (as evidenced by the completed works), Coker structures the process for learning about architectural design, environmental education, and participatory design to scaffold, meeting each student where they are and leading to great personal growth and academic learning. To complement the design studio, Coker teaches a seminar—"Designing for Equity: Ethics in the Anthropocene"—exploring poetics, ethics, and the field of public interest design. "Inherently participatory and human-centered, public interest design seeks to improve the quality of life for all people, regardless of their socio-economic background," writes John Cary, a thought leader in the field.[5] The seminar's content and series of guest speakers connect the GCDL work with the broader movement and coalition of practitioners, while making space for students to ask questions of the profession and themselves. Reflecting on the seminar and studio in combination, COOP alumna Iuliia Tambovtseva explained that these courses provided a first opportunity to engage justice and inclusion in the context of climate change within the design process. "They really made an impact on my thinking about my future in the profession and how architects have an ability to make a positive impact on the world."[6]

Within the University of Texas at Austin curriculum, the Gulf Coast DesignLab studios provide students a space to ask questions about the natural environment and professional responsibility, as they (often unknowingly) increase their environmental literacy, refine their design process, engage with ideas (that some might find far) outside the norm of contemporary practice, and reap the benefits of hands-on building. SHIFT alumnus Andy Garden reflects on his team's first day on-site on Galveston Bay:

> There's a real transformation between the idea of drawing these beautiful, smooth lines on a page and then the reality of construction. "No, there's three inches of concrete from 1950 in there, and a car fender, and you're going to have to physically dig that out." And then you need to think about the impact on the erosion on the site that you just dug out, this concrete parking lot. ... It illustrates the complexity in a way that most, if not any school projects really do.[7]

Students practice how to best present their PARTING WALL design ideas to their clients at the Corpus Christi Botanical Gardens.
© Coleman Coker

Engagement with Site and Client

Visits to the Texas coast are integral to each DesignLab studio and are strategically timed to inform the process. From the onset, students are immersed with clients in the landscape in which they work, taking the opportunity to see firsthand where and how their clients approach environmental education, land conservation, habitat restoration, and other activities. In the first portion of the semester, students travel from their Austin campus to their client's home base, taking time to get know the individuals involved, the project site, and future users. Time with the client is spent in a variety of ways, including environmental education activities, hands-on restoration projects, and touring the proposed site. During their visits, students have ventured on kayak trips through alligator-infested wetlands, planted native grasses, and assisted with clean-ups after damaging storms. The physical act of participating increases the students' understanding of the site's physical parameters, the harsh climate, and the ways future users might experience the site. During their visits, students dialogue with clients always and with future users when possible. This community engagement, broadly defined as "the process of working collaboratively with and through groups of people affiliated by geographic proximity, special interest, or similar situations to address issues affecting the wellbeing of those people,"[8] is an essential facet of the participatory design process that drives public interest design.

"It's a valuable experience in school to have real people as clients that are listening to you and working with you. Our tendency is to become removed from the end users and defining architecture for other architects to look at."

—Andrew Stone, FRAME

As a group and as individuals, the students take time to study and learn about the site. RISE alumna Sarah Bensalem recalls the benefit of exercises like writing a poem or creating a drawing or painting inspired by the place. "Later on, when we were designing, we were thinking about the essence of the site and how to integrate the structure within its environment," she says.[9] Camping at the project site is another mode of learning with cost-saving benefits often utilized in GCDL studios. It provides an immersive, intimate experience with the site and fosters relationships among the designers. For RISE alumna Nieve Tierney, "Many design courses in graduate school are super heady, never-going-to-happen designs. You feel so far removed from the actual earth... Sleeping, waking up there, eating peanut butter and jelly sandwiches—all the things that we did together are what I will remember." Tierney goes on to explain how these experiences link her to the place and make her more likely to work for its protection and conservation: "You can think about the climate crisis and get angry, but unless you really love a place you might not actually do anything about it. Having a connection to nature is really important—these lovely experiences allowed us to learn the land together."[10] Almost a decade later, it's similar experiences that stick with DUNE alumnus Whitney Peper.

> I remember being there. I remember the way that we studied was going and jumping in the ocean, wandering out onto the dunes, and having our lunch outside and feeling the night breezes. It was very much the somatic experience of being there that I have body memory now of what the Gulf Coast feels like, what the humidity is like, what the salt is like.[11]

With a commitment to the Gulf Coast, Coker has successfully shaped relationships with a range of nonprofit and governmental partners, many of them collaborating multiple times. Texas Parks & Wildlife Department (TPWD), the state agency charged with managing and conserving the cultural resources of Texas, has collaborated with GCDL on five projects in three state parks. "Each one of the projects is a different and unique experience," says JJ Fleury, a GCDL alumnus who oversees design of the TPWD park system from a planning and landscape design perspective. "A floating campsite, a group site, a wildlife viewing area ... I find them inspiring. They show what we can do with design thinking and being resourceful." Reflecting on the design process for RISE, a floating campsite at Sea Rim State Park, Fluery explains the back-and-forth communication between TPWD staff and student designers, in which learning takes place on both sides of the conversation. "The students were definitely listening and thinking through how to prevent alligators from getting on top of that float. ... It required the students to think outside the box, as well as to listen to the TPWD professionals, which resulted in a trial-and-error process."[12]

Many of GCDL's nonprofit partners have a focus on children and youth. Camp Aranzazu, a summer camp in Rockport for children with special needs, hosts two projects, HIDE and ARRIVE, both educational pavilions. Also serving young Texans, Cindy Wilems, Director of Education for Galveston Bay Foundation, believes it was very important for GCDL students to understand the future project users and how children's first-hand experiences on the bay make a difference.

> It is important for the students to understand the grand scheme of the environment and the Galveston Bay ecosystem as a whole; what they're doing in their little subwatershed and how it will affect the animals—the shrimp and the crab fish. If we can get them to this basis of understanding and get them to appreciate the ecosystem itself, then we can then go and say, "Okay, so now here are our problems, right? Let's think of some ways that we can fix them. Let's think of some actual ways—not pie in the sky, 'I need a billion dollars to do this'—but how can we individually try to address these issues?"[13]

Through in-person conversations, public meetings, and virtual discussions, students practice their engagement skills while gathering feedback. "Getting real questions is always helpful to our process," Coker explains.[14] He recalls a public event during the design process for STORE, when a community member asked a question about rust and how a proposed steel screen would weather over time.

As the students explained their hope for their design and its inherent color palette, a community member pointed out the rust would provide much much-needed iron to the prairie grasses and be beneficial, an additional strong suit of the design the students had not realized.[15] FRAME alumna Claire Townley reflects on a meeting with Artist Boat stakeholders: "We had a room full of maybe fifteen or twenty interested people listening to us present our ideas ... as architecture students, getting that feedback and really, for the first time, interacting with clients was a really good learning experience."[16]

Students install the sun shading system at DUNE for the Marine Science Institute.
© Coleman Coker

Project Origins and Programmatic Needs

A review of GCDL projects reveals a handful of repeating programmatic needs tied to the coastal environment. In most cases, clients approach Coker with a project idea in response to a specific need. For example, kayak adventures are a focus of Artist Boat's environmental education activities and require lots of equipment. Artist Boat asked GCDL students to design a structure to hold sixteen kayaks with paddles, life jackets, and arts supplies, along with a shaded gathering space for twenty-five students. That concept became STORE. In other instances, a client comes into the collaboration without a specific project in mind, and Coker works with them to develop it. TPWD Sea Rim State Park superintendent Nathan Londenberg reached out to GCDL with hopes to make the wetlands portion of the park more accessible to the public. Coker posed the idea for a floating campsite that would become FLOAT, a project that developed with tight parameters, which the students called "Nathan's non-negotiables," to ensure the project aligned with the park's mission, maintenance standards, and public safety. In all cases, Coker and client collaboratively shape the projects to ensure symbiotic outcomes, benefiting the public as students learn along the way. For students, consideration of client needs provides direct links to the natural environment. Shade is the most common request from clients, as the hot sun and Texas heat makes it challenging for staff and the public to learn and work when they are exposed and uncomfortable.

> **"People love nature, but people need their own habitat in nature. The GCDL structures are these places. We want a little bit of shade, a place to sit . . . "**
> **—Karla Klay, Artist BOAT**

"We want to make sure that we have a site that is accessible to everybody and that would make people feel comfortable," explains Wilems, GBF's director of education. "One of our main educational goals is to meet students where they are, as opposed to expecting them to meet us where we are." Meeting visitors' basic needs by providing access to restrooms, drinking water, and shade during their visits is essential to shaping this comfortability.[17]

Clients often explain their need for gathering space, which GCDL students design to accommodate other functional needs as well. With COOP, GCDL students designed a fire pit and screened eating space for twelve visitors with protection from mosquitos. Also integrating a fire pit, GATHER provides a meeting point for scout and youth groups camping in Goose Island State Park and for the public participating in the park's popular walking tours. Privacy and security are other needs often expressed by clients, with custom screening elements being a common solution. At STORE, number four rebar are used in repetition to create a secure enclosure. Whether specifically requested by the client or not, consideration of views is a common thread throughout the projects. OBSERVE and RISE were designed as elevated platforms for viewing wildlife. SHIFT and INHABIT are shaded pavilions that incorporate views to create a connection between the visitor and the landscape.

FLOAT at Sea Rim State Park remains the project with the most detailed programmatic and technical requirements. Set within a wetland site that is a forty-five-minute kayak trip from the coastline, FLOAT challenged students to grapple with structural, material, and assembly concerns—and to even debate the ethics of building anything at all in the fragile, yet harsh, environment. FLOAT alumnus Evan Gruelich recalls:

> As a studio, we took seriously the thought, "What if we didn't build anything? Was it really responsible for us to have anything out there?" Whether it's the rising level of the Gulf of Mexico or just the frequency of hurricanes, was it really the right thing for us to do to create this 7,000-pound structure with rusting steel and pressure-treated wood that was going to get destroyed in a couple of years by a hurricane? So, with research we debated as a group, and that was a really helpful step back. That is the kind of debate I brought back with me into practice.[18]

The students did decide to move forward, despite the many unknowns of working within an aquatic site that's home to a diverse range of wildlife, including egrets, herons, ducks, and alligators. "I can remember alligator-proofing was a sticking point because TPWD really, really, really did not want alligators sunning themselves on the camping spot," Gruelich recalls. "Initially, they thought there had to be a four-foot-tall fence ... we found videos of alligators crawling fences, because they can do that. Basically, we had to say: It's going to be thirty inches off the water—the chance of an alligator actually getting up there is low."[19] According to TPWD staff, the project has successfully kept the alligators at bay, but revealed another wetland resident that had been overlooked: the cormorant. Loving an elevated perspective, dozens from this sea bird population could be seen resting on the top of FLOAT's tower, blanketing portions of the campsite with excrement. Several months after construction ended, student team member Max Mahaffey returned to install a custom crown at the top of the tower to address the issue.

The conclusion of each GCDL process is often the first time students experience clients and users occupying a project they have designed. BRIDGE alumna Laura Marley Lancaster, whose project was interrupted in Spring 2020 by the COVID pandemic, shares the satisfaction of getting to meet and interact with Audubon Society of Houston volunteers: "When we were able to complete construction in March of 2021, there was a volunteer luncheon on-site, and we were all excited to be able to attend and receive thanks from volunteers and stewards. That was when it felt like the project became real: getting to interface with the users of our design."[20]

When the ribbon was cut for FRAME, a group of GCDL students, Artist Boat staff, and site users made pizzas using the pizza ovens that had been integrated into the project. "It's something I think about when I, at times, get frustrated with the profession, and it helps me to keep perspective on what it's all for," says FRAME alumnus Andrew Stone. "Seeing people using your project, enjoying it, and how it meets their needs is an important experience for students to have."[21]

Collaboration in Design

"The hallmark, in my mind, of the GCDL design process is collaboration," says BRIDGE alumnus Wellington Chew. "Design in the studio might begin individually, but it must inevitably and rapidly become a group endeavor." Many alumni note this contrast from most academic design studios. "Prioritizing team work over individual decision-making was the main difference for me," says COOP alumna Iuliia Tambovtseva.[22]

While collaboration is central, students bring their unique and individual voices to the design process. Following initial research and engagement with site and client, Coker asks each student to develop an individual design proposal. The students provide feedback and discuss preferences, incrementally compromising to merge their ideas into a collective design—or developing a handful of schemes before the entirety of the studio makes a final selection. FLOAT alumnus Evan Greulich describes the studio's design process as "wonderfully and frustratingly collaborative, much more like the real working world of architecture and making buildings, where you succeed or fail by the cohesiveness and spirit of your project team. Collectively, sacrificing our egos for the collective good of the project (and studio!) was also a fantastic lesson in humility and teamwork."[23]

The richness of collaboration is often accentuated by the diversity of the student participants and their past experiences. The course is offered as part of the Advanced Studio sequence at UTSOA, and architecture students in their final two years of study, both undergraduate and graduate, are the primary participants, though the course has also been open to landscape architecture, planning, and interior design students. It is also popular with exchange and international students. Group dialogues are therefore richer and yield a broader, collective understanding of the design problems at hand. Sometimes, this takes the form of tension between the different approaches that students from various fields or backgrounds bring to the project. In the case of DUNE, architecture students "wanted to build something," while landscape architecture students were interested in "a lower-impact design intervention," recalls Whitney Peper, who was a Bachelor of Architecture student while participating in the GCDL studio. "In hindsight, I feel like architects outnumbered landscape architects, and I think eventually they caved a little bit. I actually see that as a loss."[24] In the end, the student team built a pavilion-like structure, which was subsequently destroyed during Hurricane Harvey.

> **"It's just such a different process than I'm trained to work as a visual artist - and I'm impressed that the GCDL students can come to a design consensus. Coleman is fostering that experience to get the best work out of them as a team. I don't think people can comprehend what that might take."**
> **—Karla Klay, Artist BOAT**

Balancing Time and Budget

Geography is the primary variable in the program's one-semester process. From the UT campus in Austin, students are a minimum three-hour drive from the Texas coast, yet each semester begins with it a focus on context, site, and client. Secondary research about the place leads to an initial site visit where students look, listen, and discuss with the client. This site visit typically includes some form of hands-on service, where students learn by doing alongside their clients. Upon their return to campus, students work individually at first and then merge their designs with like-minded proposals to form small groups. Eventually, the group forms a cohesive plan or selects one design to move forward into construction, in consultation with the client and Coker. During the process, students typically return for a second site visit to test their ideas and discuss the plan with stakeholders. Input from clients, other faculty, and consultants (often a structural engineer) help students refine the designs throughout. The selected design is collaboratively refined and presented to the client for approval.

Upon approval from the client, students quickly transition into the build phase no later than the seventh or eighth week of the semester, as they determine how they will bring their conceptual design into reality by the end of the fifteen-week semester (or at worst case, with a buffer during an additional sixteenth week). This step leads to specialization within the student team, as individuals take on a range of responsibilities and leadership roles, such as detailing, material acquisition, and design lead, very much analogous to professional practice. Budget is carefully considered throughout, yet it becomes more real in this phase of the project, as students price materials and associated costs. Budgets are set at the start of the project, based on funds provided by the client, and are rarely adjusted. For completed structures, budgets have ranged from $7,000 (FLOAT) to $35,000 (STORE), a factor in shaping the overall project size from the start. Bigger budgets allow for more expensive materials and detailing, rather than fundamentally changing the design in its completed state. Material donations are one way that students have stretched available funds. At this stage, students also engage with any necessary/relevant regulatory bodies for local permitting and approvals; in past projects this has included city governments, the US Army Corps of Engineers, and TPWD staff.

The studio culminates with the construction process, a carefully choreographed sequence of events. Due to the geographic distance and the responsibilities students have with their other coursework, students have short bursts of time on-site to assemble the project, which requires the team to begin fabrication on campus. During the Fall and Spring semesters, students travel to the coast over three to four long weekends for on-site construction, while summer students typically have ten to twelve concurrent days to complete the build in the hot Texas sun.

Prefabrication adds additional layers of planning and creativity to the design-build studio format. Students work through the challenge of componentization, determining which elements of the project can be broken down, fabricated on campus, and moved to the project site. This phase often requires the production of shop drawings or similar diagrams to guide their work and the work of assisting professionals, such as structural steel frame fabricators. Students make use of the school's on-campus Build Lab and a temporary, tented workspace outside of the main architecture building to pre-assemble deck and ramp components, welded screens, and other components that will speed the assembly process. In preparation for the on-site work, students carefully plan the transportation of fabricated elements and difficult-to-find materials to the job site.

Prior to beginning their design work for SHIFT, students learn how to properly plant wetland grasses from a group of local volunteers.
© Coleman Coker

Materiality for Extreme Conditions

An element that evokes both beauty and fear, water is a primary consideration in the design process. GCDL projects are designed to withstand and function under extreme water conditions: high humidity, temporary flooding, extreme rains, and sea level rise. As students grapple with future climate predictions, they quickly reframe their relationship to water—rather than striving to keep it out, they are asked to design to accommodate water. Vertical screens and cladding are detailed so that water can move through, while balancing transparency and opacity to meet clients' needs for privacy and shade. Decks are lifted off the ground with support from pier-and-beam foundations to allow water to flow underneath.

A review of GCDL projects reveals a common material palette and assemblies. "I commented to Coleman: 'I'm noticing a vernacular here. You have similar materials, similar things happening,' " recalls Anwar Bensalem. Reflecting on site visits to past GCDL projects while participating with his wife, RISE alumna Sara Bensalem, he began to note the commonalities. "It made me realize that it's not Coleman who caused the vernacular that emerged, it was all the constraints."[25] Material palettes and assembly techniques are shaped by environmental considerations and project parameters, including budget, transportation, schedule, among other considerations. The Gulf's high salinity requires use of pressure-treated lumber to withstand harsh conditions over time. Southern yellow pine is preferred for its low cost and because of the lower carbon footprint of Texas-sourced materials. Hot-dipped steel structural components are used to combat rust's effects and to increase the lifespan of the structure. With help from a structural engineer, students design for flooding and winds up to 150 miles per hour, the strength associated with Category 4 hurricanes. Structural frames are fabricated off-site, delivered, and installed by a certified local weld shop. Concrete, a high embodied-energy material, is used minimally and most often for cylindrical footings. These footings provide the needed anchoring strength and support specified by applicable building codes, while minimizing impact on the site by limiting the amount of earth disturbed and chemical infiltration into the surrounding soil. Paints and plastics are intentionally avoided, due to their unsustainable production and maintenance requirements. (GCDL clients specifically request designs with little to no maintenance.) In addition to the most commonly used materials, students incorporate locally harvested materials in response to local conditions or to create teaching opportunities. At GATHER, students integrated oyster shells into an experimental shellcrete, after learning about its historical use at Copano Bay, a nearby abandoned seaport town. They also filled vertical gabion walls with loose oyster shells to draw attention to the material and serve as a teaching tool for the many scout and youth groups that visit Goose Island State Park.

"We had to make real life decisions that were sometimes not about concept or aesthetics, but how to pour concrete or how many screws went into the deck we'd designed."
—Victoria Carter, RESTORE

Materiality is a critical factor as students strive to create functional and low maintenance designs, knowing from the beginning these projects will receive little upkeep once deployed. "When I started off in maintenance, I saw how the coast was affecting structures in the park," says Goose Island State Park assistant superintendent Tj Hinojosa, who served as the on-the-ground contact during the construction of RISE in Fall 2016. "I'll be honest: When I saw this project get kicked off, I was very skeptical." Based on his experience at the park, RISE's material palette and the exposed connections caused him the most concern. Having seen all three projects in use over the past five years, Hinojosa reports few maintenance issues and appreciation that students considered the harsh environmental conditions in their designs. At the same time, he provided practical feedback on students' use of loose oyster shells within the gabion walls at GATHER. "Learning from experience, the oyster shells won't be something used in the future, because kids like picking up the shells and moving them. They've put them all over the place, and we find them in places that they weren't intended to be." Hinojosa reports TPWD staff have refilled the top portion of the gabion walls once before, and that they're due for another refill.[26]

PARTING WALLS students develop a low-tech method for making sho sugi ban, an ancient Japanese method of burning the surface of cedar lumber so that the scorched face acts as a long-term wood preservative.
© Wilson Hack

Leadership and Teaching

Leadership is key to the Gulf Coast DesignLab's success. Coker, as founder and faculty for the program, deserves much recognition for his insight and commitment to the process over the past decade. Coker is a well-known veteran of the architectural profession, with notable fellowships, design awards, and teaching accolades, including Harvard University Graduate School of Design's Loeb Fellowship, the American Academy's Rome Prize, AIA National Design Awards, and the Association of Collegiate Schools of Architecture 2019 Architectural Education Award. Coker brings decades of teaching experience and a history of working with underserved communities to GCDL, including his work as director of the Memphis Center for Architecture at the University of Tennessee, post-Katrina design-build studios at Tulane University School of Architecture, and engagement during the early years of Auburn's Rural Studio during his eight-year professional partnership in Mockbee Coker with Samuel Mockbee. Yet Coker is not one to tout about his past successes with the students; he remains focused on the development and future success of the program.

Coker's experience undoubtedly shapes his teaching style, and GCDL students note his direct feedback and intuitive way of shaping leaders within the studio. As BRIDGE alumna Christie Johnson explains:

> Coleman was central to this process, reining in concepts with feedback on feasibility with regard to our one-semester timeline. An expert in the field, he wasn't averse to approaching something that may be difficult to construct, but consistently drove home that we needed to be realistic in our timeline to ensure that the stakeholders wouldn't be let down by an incomplete project.[27]

"I am confident the GCDL framework Coleman has built will endure, should he ever decide to hand it off. It also has potential for expansion should other schools recognize the impact and influence of this studio."
— Christie Johnson, BRIDGE

Many alumni commented on Coker's ability to guide the process in a positive direction without making the project his own. They expressed appreciation for his "brutal honesty" delivered in a way that inspires. Alumni expressed admiration for Coker and the GCDL, without overlooking the hard work and struggles inherent in each project. "Coleman manages to inspire in a realistic way ... he creates an environment that's open and deals with the particular challenges of each project," explains FLOAT alumnus Evan Greulich. "For us, it was the immense challenge of building on the water—building a floating campsite. I think the project definitely challenged him too."[28]

Coker's leadership has fostered the longevity, reliability, and consistency of the program. He has adapted GCDL to respond to weather events, budget limitations, and pandemic interruptions, shaping design work that is relevant and helpful, while remaining committed to Gulf Coast organizations and their environmental education missions. In response to Hurricane Harvey, Coker delayed the project planned for the Fall 2017 semester to lead GCDL students on a series of weekend trips to assist in disaster aid. Dubbing the project RECOVER, Coker expanded the semester's invitation to all students and faculty within University of Texas School of Architecture to join in their hands-on efforts in Rockport, Copano Bay, and the Lamar Peninsula, Texas. Likewise, Coker and the students successfully adapted to semesters forced online due to COVID. DEMONSTRATE alumnus Charlie Weber explains: "Even within the confines of the COVID virtual learning environment, emphasis on collaborative design with both the clients and other team members made this course a standout lesson in the values of grounding the design process in teamwork and community."[29]

Now a decade into the project, Coker welcomes students into the lineage of the Gulf Coast DesignLab with visits to past projects during their trips to the coast. "Walking in the footsteps of some past class - that felt really meaningful," says Peper. "It felt like there was something being woven together that we were part of, and that our project was one thread of that."[30] Along the way, students hear the stories of how projects came to be, drawing from previous lessons learned. They expand their perspective on design possibilities, the realities of construction, and the effectiveness (and limits) of materials firsthand as they grapple with their own design challenges. They consider the lifespan of projects and the potential destruction of their designs from future weather events.

Following Coker's lead, the student designers seek out ways to teach and further environmental education through their design projects. At INHABIT, students designed small nooks and slots within the vertical walls to welcome lizards and insects, creating opportunities for environmental educators to highlight these species. FRAME alumnus Andrew Stone describes the educational intentions behind his team's pavilion, which was designed for use by middle and high school students visiting Artist Boat's Coastal Heritage Preserve.

> "We oriented [the project] on the cardinal directions, so the building itself is like a reference point for the kids learning about how to understand and navigate within the coastal prairie. It's very easy to explain: 'This way is west, this is where the sun sets, and you can measure those things against the frame of the building.' ... The project is rational and clearly structured, so you see these changes that are occurring—[it's] a kind of backdrop, or framework, through which to understand the changing ecosystem."[31]

Big Questions

The Gulf Coast DesignLab poses big questions for our profession and the design process that reach well beyond the scale and size of each semester's project. Rather than generating answers, the approach fosters more questions, more ideas, and more avenues for research. To conclude this deep dive into the ethos of the Gulf Coast DesignLab, three recurring themes are interrogated, posing thoughtful questions for the future.

Questions of time and impermanence emerge in conversations about project selection and longevity in relationship to climate change predictions (such as rising sea levels and the increased frequency of extreme storm events). As Coker explains, "I don't see the projects as permanent; I see them as twenty-year projects—maybe thirty or forty years at the max. We've never done a project more than seven feet above sea level. They'll either be underwater, or we'll need a kayak."[32] Temporality is top of mind for the students, as they consider the tidal shifts, seasonal flooding, and extreme weather events that are becoming more and more common. "There's a real tension between the solidity of the construction and the recognition of how temporary it may actually end up being, given erosion, the increasing prevalence of really strong storms, sea level rise," says SHIFT alumnus Andy Garden, whose project site lost twenty feet-five of land into the Galveston Bay over the two years following its completion. "There's a real tension between the building of things that feel permanent and the reality of retreat from a coastal site. I wonder how it's going to fare. What will it be like in ten years?"[33]

"Understanding the balance between the client and users is important. Sometimes the users' voices are quieter, so looking for them and acknowledging their place in the design process is an important step."
—Victoria Carter, RESTORE

Considering change over time is an intellectually stretching challenge, yet its impermanence is an important reality for design in the age of a changing climate. GCDL students are working in fragile, dynamic places that will see notable changes within students' lifetimes. "Losing a project is something that is challenging to face; it's like, 'Oh shit, it's gone,' " says Peper, reflecting on the destruction of DUNE by Hurricane Harvey. "If we're wanting to grapple with impermanence and grief and loss—basically not being in control—there is a real beautiful opportunity there. And then another part of me is like, 'No, don't build there; let's pull back.' It feels a little bit more like finding the new edges of where builds should happen." An early project of the program, DUNE, a pavilion-like structure at the University of Texas Marine Science Center, was swept away by storm surge and has provided a tangible feedback loop for subsequent student designs. "Of course, nature and building are inseparable, but the truth of the matter is that the ecological pavilion was destroyed in a Gulf Coast hurricane, while the landscape remains. The pavilion's absence is a strong reminder of the decisions we made—and didn't make—regarding resiliency and having a 'soft touch' on the earth."[34]

Designing for impermanence is one of many multi-generational concepts that are challenging for global society to conceive of in the present, yet one that Coker strives to make tangible by exposing students to the shifting Gulf Coast landscape. Conversations with alumni revealed a range of intentions and understanding around the concept. Some alumni focused on the built—specifics that can be physically touched and seen today. Others reflected in the context of the unseen, revealing a depth of thought and ability to contextualize their project within the broader arc of climate change. "I don't think I recognized it at that time, but you do really feel a sense of a tipping point and where we are, as a global society, in terms of climate change," says SHIFT alumnus Andy Garden. "Looking back on it now, I can definitely place that as a key moment in my own consciousness."[35]

Questions of environmental justice, particularly who has access to design strategies for a changing climate and who doesn't, were part of larger conversations about designing for clients, future users, and the public good. A focus on the Gulf Coast draws out questions around injustice, as students learn about the region and its relationship to the oil and petrochemical industries, its disproportionally high rates of cancer and human health concerns, the loss of habitat for native animal species, the increasing impacts of extreme weather events, and other pressing issues. In reflection, many alumni connected the practical and positional act of design to address social and environment problems to their career choices following graduation. "In the summer of 2020, the forces of COVID alongside BLM protests were impossible to ignore," recalls DEMONSTRATE alumnus Charlie Weber, "and couldn't have made stronger cases for the questions GCDL has always asked: Whose voices are represented in our design education and practice? And why?"[36] Others reflected on the content of architectural education itself: "Architecture school often whitewashes—and greenwashes—design, allowing studios to exist in the ether of pure form and individual expression," explains BRIDGE alumna Christie Johnson. "GCDL confronts this legacy, ensuring that even as students return to more conventional studios, they will move forward with a greater understanding of issues such as environmental racism, inequity in design, and the role the built environment plays both in the climate crisis, as well as resiliency."[37]

One way Coker and GCDL engage these issues of injustice is through client selection. Artist Boat, for example, is a Gulf Coast-focused organization and client whose environmental education programs welcome middle and high school students from the Houston area, many of whom are low-income and have not visited the coast before. With Artist Boat, this exposure to the Gulf Coast broadens students' individual perspectives, while increasing their community's collective knowledge. GCDL supports Artist Boat's work, and by association these Texas communities, by building physical infrastructure for educational programs. FRAME and STORE provide shaded space for teaching and learning activities as well as storage for the tools and equipment that enable education to take place in the coastal prairie landscape. In collaboration with groups like Artist Boat, GCDL students can help to diversify who has access to environmental education—thereby increasing resiliency and the capacity of Texas communities to develop climate crisis solutions suited to their needs.

Questions of responsibility and action lead to discussions of optimism and hope. As a community of designers and creatives, GCDL pushes back against the notion that the climate crisis is not a design problem, or is a challenge for scientists and technicians to address alone. Coker emphasizes the power of architecture as a form of activism; he teaches students that architects and designers have the knowledge and capability to embrace their collective responsibility and bring about positive change within their spheres of influence and beyond. This premise, when carried into practice, has the potential to shape an entire generation while instilling a sense of optimism. SHIFT alumna Arlene Ellwood explains:

> GCDL played a huge role in my architectural education and what I chose to do after graduating. Prior to that studio, I was feeling frustrated and disheartened by the architectural profession and was having a hard time seeing a career path where I would be able to be a part of the type of positive change that I want to make in the world. In taking this studio, I learned what participatory design can actually look like, and that is the career path I have chosen as a designer.[38]

Even in the face of challenges, this optimism sets the tone for GCDL's process and spurs exploration and engagement with the environment and stakeholders. "GCDL helped me to approach the ongoing climate crisis with a helpful, productive mindset that is neither defeatist nor naive," explains FLOAT alumnus Evan Gruelich. "GCDL taught me that, in the face of (seemingly) impending doom, the only response that passes muster is to just roll up your sleeves and keep working hard."[39] RISE alumnus Max Mahaffey offered a like-minded response that emphasizes a positive perspective on the future: "I felt more empowered to talk about the climate crisis with others after the studio, and it also made me a bit more hopeful."[40]

Drawing on this optimism, Gulf Coast DesignLab offers a model in which designers reframe their architectural work not as an end, but as a beginning. Built projects become a starting point to ask questions about the natural environment and imagine the best way forward. Nested within this hands-on approach to civic engagement, the model for education and practice addresses the needs of coastal communities by designing and building places that inspire and awaken others to their surroundings.

Developing an intimate knowledge and relationship with their surroundings provides a starting point from which practitioners, academics, and students can produce an architecture more attuned and responsive to pressing environmental needs. As shorelines shift, prairie grasses are restored, structures are washed away, and new development creeps in, these works become a measuring device for changing conditions, including those changes taking place within designers. If, like Coker, designers can begin to see their built works as a "residue" of their learning, they can continually make space to ask questions and find moments of pause that make it possible to become enamored with the planet.

Acknowledgments

Portions of this chapter were first published in "Transformation in the Age of Climate Change: Reflecting on the Gulf Coast DesignLab" and "In Motion: Exploring Context within the Design Process" in *OPEN: 108th ACSA Annual Meeting Proceedings* published in 2020 by ACSA Press.

Endnotes

1 Coleman Coker in discussion with the author, June 2019.
2 Coleman Coker in discussion with the author, June 2019.
3 Adam Hopfner, "Foreword," *The Design-Build Studio: Crafting Meaningful Work in Architectural Education*, (New York: Routledge, 2018).
4 Coleman Coker in discussion with the author, June 2019.
5 John Cary. Public Architecture. http:www.publicarchitecture.org. (site inactive)
6 Iuliia Tambovtseva (COOP Fall 2019), Response to GCDL Alumni Questionnaire, 9 October 2021.
7 Andy Garden (GCDL Alumni, SHIFT) in discussion with the author, 21 October 2021.
8 Centers for Disease Control and Prevention, *Principles of Community Engagement* - First Edition (Atlanta: CDC/ ATSDR Committee on Community Engagement, 1997), 9.
9 Sarah Bensalem (GCDL Alumni, RISE) in discussion with the author, 30 September 2021.
10 Nieve Tierney (GCDL Alumni, RISE) in discussion with the author, 2 December 2021.
11 Whitney Peper (GCDL Alumni, DUNE) in discussion with the author, 28 October 2021.
12 J.J. Fluery (Texas Parks & Wildlife) in discussion with the author, 11 November 2021.
13 Cindy Wilems (Galveston Bay Foundation) in discussion with the author, 9 December 2021.
14 Coleman Coker in discussion with the author, May 2019.
15 Coleman Coker in discussion with the author, May 2019.
16 Claire Townley (GCDL Alumni, FRAME) in discussion with the author, 12 October 2021.
17 Cindy Wilems (Galveston Bay Foundation) in discussion with the author, 9 December 2021.
18 Andrew Greulich (GCDL Alumni, FLOAT) in discussion with the author, 15 October 2021.
19 Andrew Greulich (GCDL Alumni, FLOAT) in discussion with the author, 15 October 2021.
20 Laura Marley Lancaster (BRIDGE, Spring 2020), Response to GCDL Alumni Questionnaire, 29 October 2021.
21 Andrew Stone (GCDL Alumni, FRAME) in discussion with author, 12 October 2021.
22 Iuliia Tambovtseva (COOP, Fall 2019), Response to GCDL Alumni Questionnaire, 9 October 2021.
23 Evan Greulich (GCDL Alumni, FLOAT) in discussion with the author, 15 October 2021.
24 Whitney Peper (GCDL Alumni, DUNE) in discussion with the author, 28 October 2021.
25 Anwar Bensalem in discussion with the author, 30 September 2021.
26 Tj Hinojosa (Texas Parks & Wildlife) in discussion with the author, 22 November 2021.
27 Christie Johnson (BRIDGE, Spring 2020), Response to GCDL Alumni Questionnaire, 13 October 2021.
28 Evan Greulich (GCDL Alumni, FLOAT) in discussion with the author, 15 October 2021.
29 Charlie Weber (DEMONSTRATE, Summer 2020), Response to GCDL Alumni Questionnaire, 9 October 2021.
30 Whitney Peper (GCDL Alumni, DUNE) in discussion with the author, October 28, 2021.
31 Andrew Stone (GCDL Alumni, FRAME) in discussion with the author, October 12, 2021.
32 Coleman Coker in discussion with the author, June 2019.
33 Andy Garden (GCDL Alumni, SHIFT) in discussion with author, October 21, 2021.
34 Whitney Peper (GCDL Alumni, DUNE) in discussion with the author, October 28, 2021.
35 Andy Garden (GCDL Alumni, SHIFT) in discussion with author, October 21, 2021.
36 Charlie Weber (DEMONSTRATE, Summer 2020), Response to GCDL Alumni Questionnaire, 9 October 2021.
37 Christie Johnson (BRIDGE, Spring 2020), Response to GCDL Alumni Questionnaire," 13 October 2021.
38 Arlene Ellwood (SHIFT, Summer 2019), Response to GCDL Alumni Questionnaire, 24 September 2021.
39 Evan Gruelich (FLOAT, Spring 2016), Response to GCDL Alumni Questionnaire, July 2019.
40 Max Mahaffey (FLOAT, Spring 2016), Response to GCDL Alumni Questionnaire, July 2019.

All indented quotes from GCDL alumni and clients are drawn from questionaire responses or interviews with the author.

Students finish up the steel and red cedar furniture for CANOPY at Goose Island State Park.
© Coleman Coker

Houston middle school students take part in a demonstration about water runoff pollution to help raise awareness and how they might help prevent it. The enviroscape model in use was made by students in the DEMONSTRATE studio.
© Karissa Laffey

Peering through the completed "mast" of FLOAT, a student is on alligator patrol to guard against the large reptiles spotted in the vicinity and getting too close.
© Nevin Blum

The "public" wall of RISE, sitting in a restored coastal prairie, hides the viewing platforms and ramp that look out over the wetlands of St. Charles Bay.
© Hannah Ivancie

RISE

FALL 2016

Location: Goose Island State Park

Client: Texas Parks & Wildlife Department

Design Team: Director: Coleman Coker; Students: Eric Alexander, Sara Bensalem, Mitch Flora, Hannah Frossard, James Holliday, Hannah Ivancie, Josh Leger, Max Mahaffey, Ola Olakunie, Qianhui Miao (Vonn), Michelle Sifre, Sebastian Rojas Sonderegger, Neive Tierney

Awards: 2017 ArchDaily Best Student Design-Build Projects Worldwide; 2017 American Society of Landscape Architects' national "Student Collaboration" Award; 2017 American Institute of Architects, Fort Worth chapter Student Design Award

The first time she experienced the site for RISE, an elevated viewing space for birding and educational programming at Goose Island State Park, GCDL alumna Nieve Tierney was struck by the sensory experience of the site. "I noticed the horizon line was really strong and there were different levels of colors, like bands in the horizon ... Water, grass, different kinds of shrubs, they were all really beautiful." The experience went deeper than just what she saw; Tierney goes on to describe "the sound of the bugs. You know, the loud southern Texas sound ... and it was very humid. A part of that studio that was so important was sleeping on the land, waking up early there, and getting to know it intimately in that way."[1] Like Tierney and her Gulf Coast DesignLab studiomates, Texans are smitten with the rugged beauty of the park, which draws more than 170,000 human visitors and over 450 avian species throughout the year.[2] The state park is well known for its winter birdwatching, including the sandhill and endangered whooping crane, the tallest bird species in North America, standing at over five feet tall. These rarely seen and highly protected migratory birds visit the park's wetlands in the winter season to feed on the blue crab that are plentiful during high tide. In 2019, Goose Island State Park was the winner of the annual Great Texas Birding Classic, with visitors spotting 121 species in the park on one day in April during the spring migration.[3]

In the Fall 2016 semester, Texas Parks & Wildlife Department challenged GCDL to design and build an elevated viewing space for use as an outdoor classroom for educational programming and informal use by park visitors and birders. The idea for the project arose from the work of Janelle Rand, the park's resident environmental educator, who needed a meeting place for the park's popular nature walks along the bay's edge, as well as space to teach about stewardship of wetland habitats and local bay systems. TPWD staff selected a project site within a sensitive thirty-acre habitat frequently visited by whooping crane that empties into the St. Charles Bay, land that had recently been given to the park by the Army

An opening in the wood screen expresses entry; passing through it the wetlands open up exposing views out to the waters of the bay.
© Ava Kikusaki

Prior to beginning design, students take a guided kayak tour of the bay, headed by a State Park biologist who explains the unique ecological characteristics of the surrounding area.
© Coleman Coker

Corp of Engineers in exchange for concessions to a nearby residential development. They specified that the intervention should lift visitors enough to see over the slough and wetland scrub, allowing for distant views to the bay and visiting wildlife while not deterring avian visitors. Park staff wanted the wetland areas that were physically inaccessible to become more easily viewed and, at the same time, to highlight the coastal marshland mix of plant life. The diversity of flora was of great interest to the GCDL designers, especially Tierney, one of only two landscape architecture graduate students within the studio, who made a library of the native grasses and their diverse color palette. "All of the grasses initially all look the same at first, but they're actually quite different," Tierney points out.

The dynamic environment, along with a budget of less than $10,000, drove the students' design decisions from the start. While prioritizing the needed elevation for viewing, the overall composition became a horizontal one, aligning with the local topography and echoing the distant horizon. The ninety-foot-long wood screen nestles within the native coastal grasses and partially masks the seventy-foot-long ramp used by visitors approaching by foot or car. Set obliquely to the adjacent road, the rhythmic screen is composed of simple two-by-four treated pine pieces that alternate between a parallel and perpendicular orientation in relationship to the façade. The screen's composition causes the form to appear more porous from the north and more opaque from the south, which is the common pedestrian approach from the adjacent parking lot and picnic area. The vertical dimension is diminished until visitors approach the project head on, when it becomes a backdrop for the tactile, knee-high native grasses that visually shorten its vertical dimension. A short oyster-shell path leads to a large aperture in the screen, drawing visitors into the project and framing a first glimpse of the marshland beyond. Space expands into openness as visitors move up the ramp, as the progressing elevational shift allows for views over the scrub and toward the wetland edge. The generous six-foot width of the ramp accommodates pauses for reflection and teaching, while the screen acts as a register for the vertical rise and blocks views to the parking area. At the top, an eight-foot by twelve-foot platform provides views in all directions, with the screen becoming a guardrail on the platform's western edge. On the descent, visitors can again

RISE students hike through the wetlands to which their observation platform will focus. This area is rich with blue grab, the primary food source of the endangered whooping crane that winters in this area. RISE is used to raise awareness about the highly endangered bird to the public and describe how the tallest bird in the North America is making a successful recovery.

RISE students discuss the best location to locate their project, aiming to offer prime views of the wetlands, while not jeopardizing the undisturbed visits of whooping cranes. © Coleman Coker

focus on the local flora, glimpsing marshland scrub and grasses through the steel structural frame that supports and bounds the austere intervention.

While humbly asserting its presence, RISE registers the horizontal nature of the coastline in the immediate topography and distant horizon. The award-winning design sits in juxtaposition to a recently completed McMansion-style neighborhood across the bay. Even at a distance, the collection of large, two-story homes contrasts the scale and minimalist intent of RISE, while creating an opportunity for dialogue about the built environment. When asked about the project's use since its completion in December 2016, Goose Island State Park Assistant Superintendent Tj Hinojosa speaks positively about its performance and consistent use, including as the primary meeting spot for the park's walking tours. "It is pretty neat seeing large groups take up the entire run of RISE. They spread out the entire length of it, watching out into the wetland." Hinojosa, who served as the on-the-ground park contact during the construction of RISE in his previous park ranger position, admits his initial "skepticism" of the designers' material choices and construction details, yet reports the few maintenance issues have been related to hurricane damage. Showing appreciation for the collection of completed projects in the park—GATHER, CANOPY, and RISE—JJ Fluery, a GCDL alumnus instrumental in the 2016 CULTIVATE studio—who now oversees the park system's design from a planning and landscape design perspective as TPWD planning and geospatial resources manager—explains, "The projects inspire us, for those that visit the park and myself. TPWD aims for unique designs that are responsive. The GCDL designs do that well."[4]

— Sarah Gamble

Endnotes

1 Nieve Tierney (GCDL Alumni, RISE) in discussion with the author, 2 December 2021.

2 Texas Parks & Wildlife Department, Visitation data provided to the author, 22 July 2019.

3 "2019 Birding Classic Final Results," Texas Parks & Wildlife Department, accessed 15 July 2020. https://tpwd.texas.gov/events/great-texas-birding-classic/winnersreports/2019-birding-classic-final-results_formatted.pdf.

4 JJ Fluery (Texas Parks & Wildlife) in discussion with the author, 11 November 2021.

RISE students build a model that will be used for their design presentation to the park officials.
© Coleman Coker

RISE students present their design ideas for discussion and approval.
© Ava Kikusaki

The "build" team decides how to best begin the construction of RISE.
© Sara Bensalem

RISE students place the multiple steel frames used to support the ramp and decks.
© Coleman Coker

Upon passing through the opening in the screen wall, overhead steel frames were designed to express entry, providing a contrasting experience to the more open, ninety-foot-long viewing ramp and decks.
© Coleman Coker

A RISE student puts the finishing touches on the structural steel that supports the wood screen.

So the job can stay on schedule, students work into the evening on the steel framing for the handrail system.
© Coleman Coker

A RISE student does some "outboard" welding on the steel angle and expanded metal handrail system.
© Coleman Coker

RISE students install structural members of the metal handrail system.
© Sara Bensalem

A view of the completed RISE, showing the structural steel support system and handrails.
© Coleman Coker

The steel for RISE is left unpainted to patina to a soft rust color over time and fit into the surrounding landscape.
© Ava Kikusaki

A view of RISE, showing the entry porch that visitors pass through before heading up the viewing ramp.
© Ava Kikusaki

A RISE student talks with a young visitor who asks about architects and what we do.
© Hannah Ivancie

A view of **RISE**, showing how visitors are partially seen through the screen wall on the entry side.
© Ava Kikusaki

Students from a Houston public school take a short football break after their kayak outing at the Coastal Heritage Preserve.
© Pia Navarrete Garcia

STORE

SPRING 2017

Location: Galveston Island, TX
Client: Coastal Heritage Preserve
Design Team: Director: Coleman Coker; Students: Ryan Carlisle, Emily Chaney, Clayton Cain, Sadie Dubicki, Samantha Gutteridge, Haley Lovelady, Chloe Malek, Marsden Merkle, Renica Naeva, Marriene Ondo, Alexandra Padila, Anjulie Palta, Julie Patterson, Ian Randall, Yee (Fiona) Sang Wong
Awards: 2019 City of Galveston Planning and Design Award

Located on Galveston Island, the Coastal Heritage Preserve is a 605-acre conservation area, one of the largest single-owner, contiguous pieces of land on the Island. Within the Preserve, Artist Boat, the non-profit owner, provides environmental education, including guided walks, bird watching, and kayak excursions, while working to protect and restore the undeveloped track sandwiched by development. With a focus on educating middle and high school students from Houston's inner-city neighborhoods, Artist Boat's kayak excursions provide an immersive experience for participants and have become central to their youth programming. To accommodate the growing number of student groups participating, Artist Boat needed shaded gathering and storage space. So, in Spring 2017, Artist Boat collaborated with GCDL to design its first structure within the Preserve, centered on equipment storage and gathering space for the kayak excursions.

While only a short forty-five-minute drive from the Texas coast, many Houston-based students experience the ocean for the first time on these Artist Boat excursions. Their three-hour kayak trips provide hands-on learning adventures that incorporate the arts, science, and the environment. Students traverse through the wetlands with extended stops to hear from biologists, ecologists, and master naturalists about topics like carbon sequestration ("blue carbon") and the effects of climate change, pollution, and sea level rise. While experts verbally present, the students watercolor paint what they see. Free from distraction, the students look (*really* look) at their surroundings and tap into their creativity to capture their impressions. The experience is centered on the act of observation rather than particular artistic techniques, with beautiful outcomes for all who participate.

As the program continues to grow, Artist Boat needed a more permanent place within the grasslands to store equipment and serve as a meeting place for student groups before and after the adventures. Artist Boat asked GCDL to design a secure storage area suited for sixteen tandem kayaks, life vests, paddles, watercolor paint kits, and educational tools. The structure also needed to accommodate student groups of twenty-five with a place to gather in shade and share their experiences. Locating the new structure outside of the area controlled by the Army Corps of Engineers, Artist Boat selected a site near a small channel previously dredged for use by local residents. It was the ideal spot for students to circle up and learn how to kayak on land, before plunging in.

On their first visit to the preserve, GCDL students spent time with Artist Boat executive director Karla Klay and preserve staff while walking the site and surrounding landscape. Led by the client, GCDL students took a kayak excursion of their own, becoming familiar with the wetland environment and the educational experience designed for the middle and high school-age participants. Later in the semester, Klay traveled to Austin to provide feedback on proposals before students returned to Galveston to present their final design to the Artist Boat board of directors, local preservation groups, environmentalists, and the public.

At 950 square feet, STORE is a simple, rectangular form complementing the horizontal landscape, while providing security and shade. A galvanized steel frame supports a pine structure overhead with EPDM roof membrane. Beneath the roof, the structure's east end is enclosed to create storage space, while the west end opens up to the landscape. The covered volume is wrapped by a dynamic screen of number four rebar meticulously welded by GCDL students on-campus before it was transported to the site. The screen texture is tight where security is needed on the east end and more porous to the west, framing sweeping views of the prairie. The array of linear elements recalls the native grasses in winter, which take on shades of grays and reds similar to the rusting steel. Corrugated steel sheets, left to patina, wrap the outer three faces of the fully enclosed storage space, composing a solid eastern facade. A welded rack system supports the sixteen kayaks and is secured by two sliding doors that divide the project in half. At the western end, a fully shaded elevated deck provides a seating area and frames the distant sunset for visitors.

STORE's success has led to two subsequent GCDL projects with Artist Boat: FRAME in Spring 2018 and OBSERVE, the first project designed for public use, in Fall 2018. In 2019, the City of Galveston recognized STORE with a Planning and Design Award, placing the GCDL design among those projects completed in the past five years that "contribute to a better quality of life in our community and serve as models to learn from and emulate."[1]

— Sarah Gamble

Acknowledgments

An earlier version of this project description was first published in "Transformation in the Age of Climate Change: Reflecting on the Gulf Coast DesignLab" in *OPEN: 108th ACSA Annual Meeting Proceedings* published in 2020 by ACSA Press.

Endnotes

1 "Planning Awards", City of Galveston Planning and Development Division, accessed 15 November 2021. https://www.galvestontx.gov/1107/Planning-Awards.

Students present their design ideas for the new kayak / outdoor education facility for STORE.
© Coleman Coker

STORE students review a mockup proposal for the perimeter screens, made of common #4 steel rebar. This size steel is typically used for concrete reinforcing, but its use at STORE is out of the ordinary.
© Coleman Coker

STORE students present their design proposal to their clients.
© Coleman Coker

STORE students place concrete for the structural steel frame foundation.
© Coleman Coker

Students work late to catch the sunset looking through the structural steel frame.
© Henry Yamamoto

STORE students prepare for the structural wood roof framing.

STORE student install structural wood blocking between joist members.
© Coleman Coker

A group of students from a Houston-area school are about to take their first kayak trip.
© Pia Navarrete Garcia

A view of the steel rebar on the exterior of the structure, showing how the density of the members increase in the area where the kayaks are stored.

A student welds the steel supports where the kayaks are stored.
© Coleman Coker

The rebar screen and cor-ten steel sheathing applied to the storage structure have a rich, red patina.
© Henry Yamamoto

STORE students install framing and the plywood roof deck.
© Coleman Coker

Artist Boat staff and visiting middle school students prepare the kayaks for a trip on Galveston Bay.
© Coleman Coker

A view of **STORE** from the Coastal Heritage Preserve, with one of its wetlands in the foreground.
© Henry Yamamoto

Visitors head toward **STORE** in preparation for a winter kayak outing.
© Henry Yamamoto

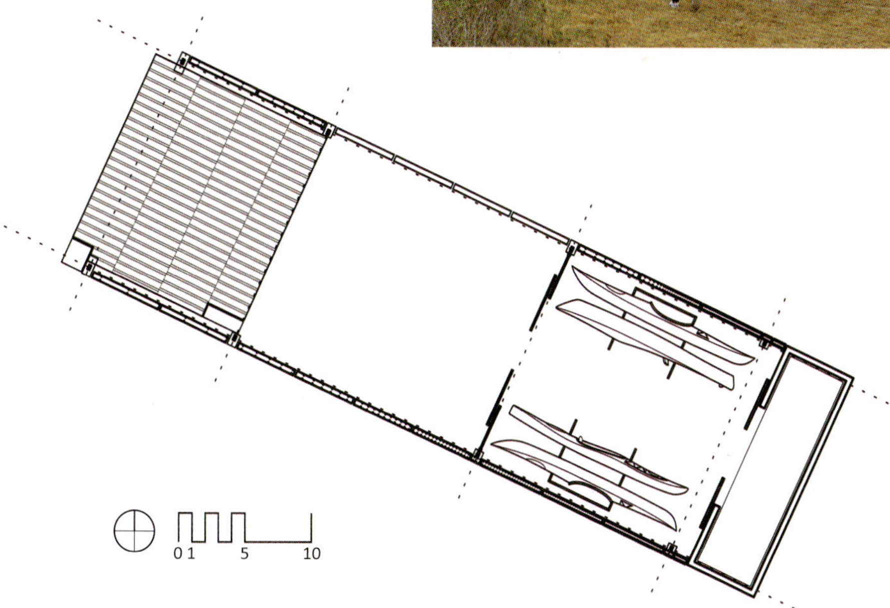

Middle school students at FRAME share their impressions after a walk through the coastal prairie at Galveston Island's Coastal Heritage Preserve.
© Mary Warwick

CHAPTER 3

Act as If Your House Is on Fire

Coleman Coker

Small Acts Change the World

"I want you to act as if your house is on fire. Because it is." These words from Greta Thunberg have been burned into our collective consciousness. When she spoke them at the World Economic Forum in 2019, she was a sixteen-year-old climate activist who spoke out not only on behalf of her generation, but for all of us. Her words did more to awaken the world to the ecological emergency than any politician or established environmental group ever has. The immediacy of her sharp message challenges us to act now, before it's too late.

How are we, as designers, responding to Greta's call for action? Are we acting to extinguish such an unfathomably huge fire? Are we acting in a way that points us to a brighter future? It is pretty clear that we are not on the frontlines leading the way. We barely even sound the societal alarm about what many see as unprecedented upheaval and loss. Many of us bury our heads in the sand, knowing full-well the future is in certain jeopardy. Due to inaction, we carelessly pour fuel onto the blaze. The upheaval whole nations are beginning to face—especially among the world's poorest—brought on by this ecological emergency, is reshaping the world in ways we don't yet understand. The world is in tumult and it's only going to intensify. Yet many still don't connect the dots.

With increasing social turbulence, rising temperatures, melting ice, and burning forests, little has changed in the way that design has been taught through the last half-century. Architecture studios, for the most part, are still sequestered in the ivory tower of academia, far from the messiness of change and disruption happening outside its walls. In most schools, the "starchitect" is still held up as *the* model to which students should aspire. Pedagogies fixate on formal aesthetic concerns that only society's most affluent can afford. As barbarians crash through the gates, we insist on assigning design problems relevant only to that very narrow spectrum of the world's financially elite. Does a family in Bangladesh, whose farmland has been flooded by rising oceans, concern itself about whether the next cultural museum in Dhaka is made of concrete or stainless steel? Do over-burdened mothers in The Tre of Houston, working three jobs to make ends meet, anxiously await a glimpse of the cutting-edge three-million-dollar addition to the already six-million-dollar residence across town in River Oaks? We designers need to open our eyes and see that this vision of a bigger, brighter, shinier city filled with more shape-shifting building designs is irrelevant at best. More disconcerting though, is that this vision is damning to our students' futures because it puts them so out of touch with the rest of the world.

We designers need to reimagine the roles architecture can play in communities—new roles that will make us more relevant and realistic—how we might better shape and support resilient neighborhoods and cities, shelter those in need, and safeguard our disappearing ecological systems. A good place to start would be to recognize the consequences of our actions, both immediate and long-term, and to cultivate the art of listening. That's because we architects are bad listeners; we feel we already know the answer before we've heard the question. First, we must learn how to listen and after, learn how to respond to those we've heard by giving them what they really need, instead of telling them what they should want. As we learn to listen better, becoming brave enough to ask broad, inclusive questions, we can then begin to shape a new narrative where we become more forward-thinking, holistic-minded designers. As we open our collective eyes to what's happening all around—inequality, impoverishment, the danger of threatened ecological systems—we'll be better prepared to reimagine our role. We can become professionals that support the communities in which we work, stewards standing ready to protect the ecological systems on which we rely. We can begin by working in embedded ways, by using the resourceful imaginations we possess in ways that will benefit everyone. That reimagined role would be based on humility and respect, on caring about those we work with, on learning from them to fashion a broader perspective to benefit them and their children, and their children's children yet to come.

"I learned most about the climate crisis in our ethics seminar. Greta Thunberg was becoming very vocal with her activism and we studied her goals and ideas; an important awareness to have as we learned to contribute to the built environment."
—Natalie Avellar, COOP

Our new story can be shaped around building community relationship, where design students and teachers might see architecture more as an ontological investigation, one that helps us better understand who we are, why we are, what our relationship to the world is, and how we can better ourselves by critically questioning that relationship. This would mean leaving our ivory tower and venturing into public space, and seeing, feeling, smelling, and tasting the real world, allowing us to better recognize what a more viable role in that world might be. This would provide an interdependent scholarship, one that would encourage students to experience the world in an ecologically-based way, what Timothy Morton calls "ecological thought."[1] I'm using the textbook definition of ecology: the relations of organisms to one another and their surroundings. The many parts of what we call the world—whether the city of New York, a table fork, a weekend cottage by the sea, our national expressway system, the carbon we pump into the air, every living thing in the Brazilian rain forest, the chair you're sitting in right now, and ourselves—are interconnected to make an ever-shifting, always-becoming whole. We can learn to make connections between its many parts, starting with our own world-relationship, and expanding that to include each other and the surrounding environment[2], our home, this planet.

RISE students research and document boardwalk wetlands at Sea Rim State Park. © Coleman Coker

Using quick study models, students from CULTIVATE get feedback from neighbors who will use the finished project. © Coleman Coker

Students present their landscaping ideas for CULTIVATE in East Austin.

A student who shapes herself as being part of this greater interconnected world gains the ability to step back from the narrow lens of "Big-A" architecture, institutionalized and entrenched in exclusivity, to imagine a broader perspective that accounts for the whole. With that, she can ask how others might better interact with the wider world through the buildings she designs and the cities she shapes. This is architecture as a living, breathing, active verb instead of—no matter how aesthetically pleasing—a static, lifeless noun. Living this story, our young architect learns to shape an all-encompassing action-architecture, embracing inclusion and equity—fashioning beauty for everyone. Instead of peering in from the outside, she stands inside "community"—and by *community*, I mean all beings—becoming an integral part of it, contributing to others' well-being. Living a "small-a" design approach opens her to the larger interconnected world, so that it becomes foundational to her new narrative, a new story, in which she is awakened to wonder.

This is the story I want students to take away from the academy, to retell it in their own way, adding their own experiences to the tale. This is an inclusive and affirmative story that encompasses the whole of humanity and everything else. It is a tale in which students want to make places of beauty for others, of nurturing and safeguarding the world, a narrative in which they might discover a connection to something larger than themselves. This ought to be part of everyone's collective story that gives us a sense of belonging and to which we're unequivocally invested, that maintains and preserves ourselves, others, and everything that is.

A tall order no doubt, one that might even sound naïve, or like too much to take on. But our lives are shaped around the narratives we learn and retell. We each have a personal story to tell, while being part of a collective cultural story. We all add to that larger collective, so it is constantly in flux, being reshaped to tell itself anew. By crafting a story of inclusion instead of exclusion, of listening instead of telling, of being part of a community instead of a self-appointed elite, we begin to understand we are not just individuals reimagining and reframing the narrative alone, but many who desire long-overdue change. This new reality is already taking place, being felt in communities around the world, coming to the forefront more each day. Many are crafting their own new stories to bring about significant change through grassroots efforts, working in small local groups, banding together to make better communities for themselves and their neighbors. As Howard Zinn said, "Small acts, when multiplied by millions of people, can quietly become a power no government can suppress, a power that can transform the world."[3] These millions of small acts aren't waiting on governments, universities, or big business; no authority is organizing them. Those who are concerned about what they see are the new generation of volunteers rolling up their sleeves, one by one, to collectively work for change. This loosely-linked confederation is about mutual partnership, about the fundamental desire to make a better place for everyone. Through our collective small acts, we designers can and should be part of this emerging narrative. If we choose to become part of this collective groundswell, we can, like Greta—just one persistent teenage girl—learn to speak out for change. Doing so, we'll begin to see ourselves as part of the ecological whole, discovering relationship with the world and its many parts. Each of the small acts we perform adds to the collective whole to make the world a better place for all.

A young student uses a field microscope to examine tiny sea life. Note the plasma cut relief map of Galveston Bay, which faces out toward it.

FRAME students get feedback on their design proposal from the stakeholders they are working with that semester.

Woven From Hope

With cities slowly drowning, landscapes charred beyond recognition, mounting displacement of whole cultures, fewer and fewer resources for so many, the poor getting poorer, the slow-moving deaths of millions in the global south, we designers—and everyone else for that matter—must quit referring to what is happening as "climate change," and call it what it is: an ecological emergency. Climate change refers only to one aspect of the breakdown we're causing. It doesn't directly address habitat loss, topsoil depletion, increasing plastic pollution, rainforest reduction, clean water scarcity, species extinction, collapsing fisheries, and more. We have told ourselves for too long that we are indeed the masters of our planet, that the natural world is our vast *smörgåsbord*, waiting to be picked clean, and that it's all right if our short-term desires win out over long-term consequences. Framing our relationship to the world in this manner alienates us, blinding us to the destruction we have done. The climate emergency, which affects every living being on the planet, is our doing and ours alone. The "haves" have a deep moral responsibility to the "have nots" to rectify this, and to work toward rectifying all that caused this calamity in the first place. A more caring narrative that expresses our relationship with the world built on mutual respect, compassion, our innate need for beauty in our lives, and the kind of care that engenders meaningful cooperative relationships with one another and with the environment on which we depend, can turn around this undoing and generate a deeper sense of belonging.

This deep-seated sense of belonging to something greater than ourselves is in our genes, according to E. O. Wilson. He calls this sense of connection "biophilia" and describes it as an affection for living things, love of life, and love for living natural systems: "The innate tendency to focus on life like processes ... to affiliate with life is a deep and complicated process in mental development ... our existence depends on this propensity, our spirit is woven from it, hope rises on its currents."[4] Consider the losses happening all around us that deserve our full attention. We can learn to care for what we're losing by acknowledging the abiding love that is an essential part of our forgotten story. Rekindling this will open our hearts to caring for the world, for looking after it better, if we want future generations to have long, full lives. Design approaches that express this inborn affection for life help us live more connected lives and compel us to act in ways that do no harm.

The kind of change that Wilson describes—respect and love of life—begins with each of us. It is a way of changing how we relate to the world that reap relational benefits. Embedding biophilia deep into architectural discourse may at first seem difficult, but it is a desire that's already part of us. After all, we designers don't really create anything. Instead, we borrow that which is already of this world and rearrange it into things we recognize as buildings, bridges, lounge chairs, and lamps that were once "nature." Biophilia simply invites us to see that when we design something, that rearrangement is an expression of love, an affection embedded in us, unencumbered by bias or hesitation, not overwhelmed with our own self-importance. Once that love is acknowledged, care will follow: care for the things we make, care for others and for all life. By weaving love into the tale we tell, we reorient and transform our design approaches into a more holistic enterprise.

Change like this can happen. It would be transformational, and I believe it can happen through the upcoming generation, of which our students are a part. It begins with the courage of each individual, and then in seeking out like-minded people with whom to share the work of making the world better. Biophilic love can be expressed in many ways; it can be the origin of "beautiful" design, where an ecologically-based, community-driven design begins. In the Gulf Coast landscapes—coastal prairie, ocean edge, back bay and their abundance of flora and fauna—in which we work, we are closer to *life* and the opportunity to recognize what biophilic affection might mean. Love of life is already manifested in the students' work and in their affirmation toward a better future. Nurturing this in each student is just one way—and there are many—of changing the design education narrative.

"I felt hyper-aware of my surroundings at our site; I began to notice things that were always there but had never paid attention to, like what types of birds congregate in certain areas at certain times and how things were always changing based on the time of day and year."
—Laura Marley Lancaster, BRIDGE

More specifically, Gulf Coast Design Lab (GCDL) students respond to biophilia through designing and making places where one can realize a firsthand relationship with their surroundings. Over ten years and through twenty-five projects, our students have designed appropriate places for the public that not only accommodate but also inspire. Many of the projects they have done have been for middle- and high-school students from underserved neighborhoods, many of whom live in environmentally compromised communities. Using the places that our DesignLab students have designed and constructed, science-based professionals, biologists, ecologists, and artists involve these middle- and high schoolers in field-based, educational experiences meant to increase their ecological literacy.

Those working with students from elementary to high school will tell you that students retain more of what they learn when there is physical activity involved, instead of just being engaged in passive classroom activities. Giving the public engaging outdoor places to learn about their environment can be a life-changing experience and provide them with a broadened perspective of who they are and what they can do. GCDL-designed spaces have given environmental educators the opportunity to hold demonstrations about local ecological conditions and to instill a deeper sense of stewardship and responsibility by offering hands-on experiences. GCDL students have built observation platforms from which to watch wildlife; shade structures for hosting eco-demonstrations; and facilities for hands-on teaching, dining, and even potting native prairie grasses. They have built places for others to sit around a fire to hear stories. They have designed and constructed screened living rooms to find shelter from mosquitos, and field stations for middle- and high-school students to test water samples for unhealthy contaminants or marvel at tiny sea creatures, which can only be seen with the aid of a microscope. GCDL students have made structures for close-up observation and education about coastal prairies and efforts to reestablish them, wetlands where volunteers have worked to slow their retreat by renourishing them with newly-planted sea grasses and bay edges where a lone osprey circles overhead and pods of dolphin breach the water's surface. These outdoor spaces give educators places to teach about the harm brought to waterfowl by biomagnification, demonstrate the effects of beach erosion through hands-on exercises, or explain the injury done to estuary wildlife by illegally-spilled pollutants. These are just a few of the activities offered to kindergarten-through-high-school students and the public alike, helping improve their ecological understanding of the places where they live. These outdoor places are meant to offer the public not only the beauty found within their work but the opportunity to build a relationship with their local environment, so that through firsthand experiences they realize the importance of strong, healthy ecological systems; the increasing risks brought on by our eco-emergency; and, in turn, learn how-to environmental stewardship practices meant to help offset the ecological crisis. The work our DesignLab students do is indeed one expression of biophilic love, articulated through their environmental activism meant to make the world a little bit better.

"I definitely came into the GCDL with an awareness of the climate crisis, yet as we watched our project site erode before our eyes it felt much more tangible. At the same time, we were learning about our client's care in mitigating the effects of the climate crisis, then sharing that hope with us."
—Arlene Ellwood, SHIFT

Community-based work like this benefits our architecture students in many ways. It's inspirited pragmatism shapes their design skills by working with real-world clients so that a project is not just an isolated exploration in technique and theory but is in fact real, tangible work that affects people's lives. These experiences expand our students' understanding about their future roles as designers by challenging their accustomed notion of architects sequestered in offices behind computers developing their top-down designs. Through the engaged work they do with their stakeholders, GCDL students learn on the job by helping local citizens understand more about their local ecological systems and how to better protect them. Their work even helps empower local citizens to demand change from corporations and insist on equity for those being harmed. Working directly with community groups helps our students craft their own habits of empowered action. Helping others this way increases our students' self-confidence and adds to their self-worth. They learn how rewarding it is to make change happen.

As they learn about design this way, the contributions they make expand their ethical horizons. Their lessons in ethics come through environmental activism, by experiencing the practical good of serving the citizens of the communities in which they work—doing unto others as you would have them do unto you. These experiences offer the opportunity for reflection, which can inspire a student to make the world a bit better in everything they set out to do. And while the work the GCDL students do increases public ecological literacy, just as importantly, it is aimed at them. Their initial research before the process begins gives them a deep appreciation and respect for the ecology of where they will be working. They also learn about ecological relationships from the same environmental educators with whom they work in ways that nurture their own biophilic attraction, which helps them develop their own ecological way of thinking. Through the work they do, not only do they design and make an outstanding building, they take part in something greater than themselves, participating in a tiny way toward a brighter future, a more hopeful future, for them and for others.

Students help clean up after Hurricane Harvey by removing a fallen tree from a structure at Camp Aranzazu, where HIDE was previously constructed.
© Coleman Coker

Students from CULTIVATE discuss their design drawings with a neighbor who will use the finished project.
© Coleman Coker

Empowered Activism Empowers

Engaging the community, as GCDL students do, demands not only new skill sets, but also consideration about what should be an essential part of an architect's education: ethics. Considering the responsibilities architects have to the communities in which they work—particularly to poorer, underserved areas that have never benefitted from the involvement of architects—ethics are essential. Bundled within ethics are issues of equity, environmental justice, racism, and environmental ethics our students learn about through the non-profits they partner with, they also have that opportunity though formal and informal discussions in studio and seminar. More formal discussions are held in a seminar that I teach each semester—"Designing for Social Equity: Ethics in the Anthropocene"—where we research and discuss the ethics of environmental racism and ecological responsibility. Some of our discussions center around ethical accountability and the fact that the more affluent a person is, the larger their carbon footprint, the effects of which disproportionally affect the disempowered who suffer most from our climate crisis. Often those affected most have contributed least to the overabundance of atmospheric CO_2; they are more likely to starve, die of thirst or disease, or be forcibly displaced due to the changing climate. GCDL students have researched opinion polls to find that people of color who are often disproportionally disempowered are understandably more concerned about a shift in climate norms, since they have more to lose. Through research like this, students become more aware of how affluent citizens such as themselves are much more likely than poorer citizens to have homeowner's insurance, and are therefore more protected if their homes are damaged or destroyed by a hurricane, for example. If wildfires ravage the landscape, those with higher incomes have the means to evacuate, because they own vehicles. Those less affluent left behind in New Orleans as Hurricane Katrina bore down on the City didn't own vehicles; they had no financial means to leave or even to get across town to find shelter. Like them, the poor everywhere suffer the consequences.

Focusing on the Gulf coast, GCDL students have found that environmental racism is a dividing factor, an inequitable reality for so many. Since equity should play a substantial role in how architects regard their fellow citizens—whether working with them or not—students who take my studio are asked to also take my seminar, where we think about and discuss these ethical relationships. Delving into what the ethical designer's role must be in this time of climate crisis means more than just designing comfortable and smart buildings. We discuss how to become better listeners and better facilitators, going well beyond just what it takes to design the material aspects of buildings. Drawing from public-interest-design principles, a larger ethical role of designers would begin with helping build community strength through cooperation; building advocacy groups that demand better public services; building skills so that citizens can organize community gardens, learn composting, or effectively recycle trash. An ethical charge is about uniting neighbors so they get together on a Saturday morning to plant sea grass along eroded bay edges, or re-establish oyster beds to help reduce erosion, enabling their communities to be safer when the next hurricane hits. Besides being good building designers, discussing and then putting into practice these considerations help our students along the path to becoming ethical architects.

"This wetland is important to our park, providing an avenue for whooping cranes and sandhill cranes. RISE offered an educational perspective for our visitors because one can see things from the project that can't be seen from anywhere else in the park."
—TJ Thinojos, Texas Parks & Wildlife

Not only for themselves, DesignLab students also gain the satisfaction of helping others achieve equity through the work they do. Many of the kindergarten-through-high schoolers who benefit from GCDL's work come from homes that are underserved, underpaid, and suffer disproportionately from environmental injustice or climate events. Through better education about their local ecological conditions and better training in conservation habits via the projects that our GCDL students produce, coastal citizens gain greater empowerment to protect their homes, communities, and environment. With increased respect for their environment, these citizens are armed with the tools to act, to advocate for cleaner air in their neighborhoods, and to demand clean drinking water and restored brown fields. Through increased ecological literacy, they know that healthier wetlands and estuaries, reestablished coastal prairies, and vibrant sand dune systems make them safer from the ravages of a hurricane's force. With a greater understanding of environmental degradation and healthy ecological systems, they appreciate how healthier surroundings are crucial. Learning about ongoing environmental degradation helps them overcome systemic poverty, because it increases their demand for change. While this kind of hands-on learning is important for everyone, it can be vital for underserved, inner-city neighborhood kids. With knowledge comes power, and with power comes action.

Raised environmental awareness through increased education is a chief way to motivate communities, so they can set out to right environmental-justice wrongs, while giving them a fighting chance to stay healthy and safe. Environmental awareness, often learned through non-profit programming via organizations our students work with, helps to inform people in these communities and to make better places to live. This is what environmental activism is all about: our students playing their part in increasing ecological literacy by designing and building places and tools for environmental educators. Our GCDL students not only help empower communities, they themselves become empowered, feeling greater confidence that they can make the world more just. In doing so, they may learn to love that world a bit more, cherishing it for what it is, while working to heal it for the good of all.

Community engagement in real-world situations teaches students more than just how to be a good designer. While not on any particular pedagogical checklist of an architecture school's curriculum, their experience in hands-on work teaches students self-reliance. When working with community stakeholders, students are thrown into the breach of everyday relationship. As in any real-world relationship, things sometimes go wrong, things that have to be quickly resolved with positive outcomes. Being responsible for designing and then building the beautiful and sturdy places that will be used by their stakeholders gives students new and never-experienced challenges in which to work, where they quickly learn to rely on their best knowledge of the moment. Seeing the community benefit from their efforts gives them self-assurance in their on-the-job resourcefulness. What they gain in that will be indispensable in their post-university work.

A second asset they gain, especially when they work with community members who have seemingly intractable concerns, is mediation skills. When roadblocks occur, students, as outsiders, can play the negotiator's role to resolve differences and help to move things forward for the greater good. A third skill gained from this method of learning is patience. Challenging situations with community groups inevitably arise. In these unpredictable circumstances, students certainly learn to practice endurance and tolerance, but oftentimes patience is the most important thing they can bring to the table. Understanding that it takes time to move things diplomatically forward, their patience can help turn the situation around and generate positive outcomes. A fourth skill gained when students are interacting with community is making decisions that rely on their intuitions. They quickly learn to trust their instincts, which cannot be generated in a theoretical design laboratory setting. Knowing in your gut what the best thing to do is in a given situation with others is something that comes only through experience. Intuition is a recognized talent in the best designers and is invaluable in school. Being confronted with situations that have no easy answers, sometimes it is only intuition that will lead to a positive outcome. The fifth characteristic that students gain is humility, particularly when they work with those most in need. Seeing themselves in relation to others in real need will definitely instill humility rather than an attitude of ascendency implicitly taught in many design education settings. And while a competitive design studio may not prove the best place to be modest, students working cheek-to-jowl with stakeholders, with whom they would likely never have worked otherwise, puts into perspective the gift of privilege they have; this can be an eye opener and have a lasting impact a student will carry with them through life. And, when engaging with communities, a sixth understanding gained is the necessity to work within limits—resolving tight material budgets and short timeframes for the projects in which our students are involved. In the world of practice, budget and time greatly impact what any designer can do. Limitations, if imaginatively handled, make the work more fitting to the conditions at hand and ultimately better. Students typically don't learn this in school through their hypothetically-driven design investigations that have no budget and few imposed limits. Through the experience of firsthand, community-driven work, limitations come

"The studio shifted my attention from designing based on visuals to experiences, instead to focus on how people would use and experience our project, rather than how it looked in a drawing."
—Joseph Hernandez, INHABIT

into play as beneficial shapers of good design. Our students gain these attributes by learning to listen to their clients, which teaches them to ask good questions, to maintain an open forum for discussion, and to gather in-depth understanding of what the right direction will be from which to begin their design process.

Equal to all these though, is the opportunity for students to find deeper relationship with the beauty of the world. Outdoor space, what we commonly call the "natural" world, is becoming increasingly unfamiliar to many university students—to most of us in fact. For most of us have spent the majority of their lives isolated in enclosed spaces artificially lit, heated and cooled, and fashioned by the lowest common denominator, all the while focused on a small screen that mesmerizes us right out of the reality of the world. My generation is the first that chose to cast off our intimate relationship with the earth, and now we have passed that detachment on to this next generation. Because of that, much has been lost. Many students sense this loss but have no words to describe it. They search without knowing for what they search. For we come to know ourselves through the places in which were brought up; one particular landscape shapes those who grew up in it and is different from others brought up in a different place. That sense of identity—the temporal and spiritual quality gained from that place—needs resuscitation. Part of the work of the GCDL program asks students to look deeper, to try and find that lost intimacy with the earth's beauty—and through that discover themselves. Beauty, of course, is such an overused word, to the point that it's lost much of its meaning. But stepping into wetlands and watching a small crab scoot past, running a hand over the smooth grasses of a coastal prairie, kayaking in a shallow back bay, squinting from the bright summer sun while feeling the heaviness of clouds overhead—and the humidity they bring—has the potential to awaken students to an unfamiliar world many have never spent much time in. This awakening can open students to what the world offers, curing them of detachment from the "flesh" of the world, and make them more attuned designers, since they can better apprehend the fullness of that world in which they will design. Working in the field as they do, they experience that corporeal relationship, such as when they need shade from the unbearable heat of the hot August afternoon, or the sensate quality of hiking through tall prairie grasses, the grittiness of sand that found its way into the boot and rubbing against a bare foot, or the cool water splash of a kayak paddle drawn through briny water. How can one expect to make beautiful things, if their only idea of beauty is projected on a laptop computer screen? In our image-addicted culture, beauty is not had by experiencing beautiful static objects—or even worse, pictures of beautiful static objects—but rather in building an active relationship with the interrelated wholeness that is all around us, what we call the earth. Heidegger described this sort of relationship in his use of the word *Dasein*,[5] where our active participation—being-in-the-world—makes it aware of itself, and through that, we become part of that activated world that comes to life and sustains us. Getting out into the landscape, students are offered the occasion to become mindful of the place

Think Ecologically

Our students do their best work when they slow down, look deeper, focus on the long-term, and embrace the fact that everyone does better work when they cooperate to achieve a common goal. This process begins with asking "what is" of the world instead of deciding "what it ought to be." It takes into account the rhythms of life, instead of working against them. GCDL students are encouraged to look deeply at when and where to build, and when and where not to build; to imagine how to design in ways that actually support ecological systems, flowing with natural cycles, instead of armoring against them. This work is about our students learning not only to do no harm to the environment, but to reach out and help others, improving the places in which they live and work. They are encouraged to become deeply suspicious of the notion "just because they can" and to instead inquire "should they?" It is also about embracing an attitude that takes into account long-term consequences. When received as a whole, these attitudes can lead to a design approach built around moderation as a first principle, embracing a "small is beautiful" view, being open to change and designing for it, designing with the whole in mind but favoring its parts, understanding that humility is the only possibility if we plan to survive. This approach takes into account the interdependence of all that is. Learning that is an important lesson for young designers who are encouraged to make these connections in the work that they do. This adds up to a kind of ecological thinking, and draws much from Timothy Morton's writing.

Timothy Morton's *The Ecological Thought* begins:

> The ecological crisis we face today is so obvious that it becomes easy—for some, strangely or frighteningly easy—to join the dots and see that everything is interconnected. This is the ecological thought. And the more we consider it, the more our world opens up ... The ecological thought doesn't just occur "in the mind." It's a practice and a process of becoming fully aware of how human beings are connected with other beings—animal, vegetable, and mineral. Ultimately, this includes thinking about democracy. What would a truly democratic encounter between us truly equal beings look like, what would it be—can we even imagine it?[7]

Learning to reach out and care for others—and everything—begins with understanding that we are all one, and that any harm one brings about comes back to harm them. This recognition opens a space where a new narrative might emerge. It is an inclusive way to understand one's place in the world. It is meant to encourage goodwill through our actions, no matter how great or small they are. This is the crucial recognition for students—and all of us—to consider in our current moment.

Thinking and acting ecologically this way simply means that one can make the world better by relating to everything in it as an interrelated whole. Practicing this sort of interdependence may define what the deepest sense of beauty can be in today's world. GCDL students are encouraged to develop an attitude built around that and based on their lived experiences and non-prescribed reflection that questions customary dogma. Students know it takes insight and courage to step off the accustomed path and venture down new ones. They understand it is about setting aside the conventional design thinking they've grown accustomed to and working in ways to make better places that inspire respect and awe of our world so that those who use those places will want to protect and safeguard it, for everyone and everything. If our students gain anything in the GCDL, my hope is that they learn how to reflect on the reality of the world of beauty beneath their feet, above their heads, and in their hearts in ways that cause them to inquire more earnestly about what they do and how it is interconnected to everything else and through that insight learn to make places that are not just better, but that are sacred for all.

"The structures help integrate art and science at the Coastal Heritage Preserve and what the GCDL students learn there through their unique coastal experiences provide them a firsthand ecological education and inspiration."

—Karla Klay, Artist Boat

If we are going to make it, we need to become aware of—and value—our home, this necessary Earth. This means finding new ways to work that respect one another, the community, and the environment—ways that enlarge our worldview and encompass equity while lending a hand to others who can use our help. As an educator, my hope is that the students I teach become better Earth citizens. I believe this can be achieved not strictly through traditional education, but through a transformed worldview that encourages well-being for all. Frankly, my generation has failed miserably at this. Our focus has been on personal independence and success of the individual. We have neither nurtured a society built on altruism or egalitarianism, nor have we recognized we are all in this together. It is our student's turn, now. They realize their hope for a better future has been compromised. They demand change. They are deeply dissatisfied with how things are in the world, with how we unfairly treat one another and this planet. They are put off by the inequity they see in their hometowns and the way poor people around the world are discarded and deemed expendable. They are alarmed by the mounting harm being done to every living thing on the Earth and in the oceans. They know there must be a better way. They want change; they demand something more than the broken promises my generation has left them. Their passionate dissatisfaction drives them to become real agents for change. In the end, they are our only hope, and we don't have much time to extinguish this house on fire.

Endnotes

1 The word "environment," falls short when describing that which we are part of. Environment, as its name infers, refers to our surroundings, the physical world, something out there beyond us—that which is not us, giving the impression that we are contained *in* something or that that condition is outside us, around us, but *not* us. Yet, environment is not around us, for we are inseparably woven into it and even more than inter-connected, we and environment are one and the same. I particularly want to point this out since "environment[al]" is part of this book's title.

2 E. O. Wilson, *Biophilia*, (Cambridge, Massachusetts and London, England: Harvard University Press, 1984) 1.

3 Timothy Morton, *The Ecological Thought*, (Cambridge, Massachusetts and London, England: Harvard University Prss, 2010).

4 Howard Zinn, *A Power Governments Cannot Suppress*, (San Francisco: City Lights Books, 2007) 47.

5 Martin Heidegger, *Being and Time*, translated by John Stambaugh, (Albany, NY: State University of New York Press, 2010).

6 Maurice Merleau-Ponty, *The Visible and the Invisible*, translated by Alphonso Lingis, (Evanston, Illinois: Nortwestern University Press, 1968).

7 Timothy Morton, *The Ecological Thought*, 1-7.

All indented quotes from GCDL alumni and clients are drawn from questionaire responses or interviews with Sarah Gamble.

GCDL students pour concrete for the new fire circle project IGNITE, which will be used by the San Jacinto Girl Scouts.
© Coleman Coker

GCDL students lay terra cotta block (turned on edge to let breezes pass through) for a screen wall at IGNITE on Galveston Island.
© Coleman Coker

GCDL students test out IGNITE, a new fire circle gathering area and monarch butterfly waystation they just completed for the San Jacinto Girl Scouts at their new property on Galveston Island.
© Coleman Coker

Nestled between native Yaupon Holly, a view of INHABIT from the bay side showing the western shade screen.
© Avi Greene

INHABIT

SUMMER 2016

Location: Galveston Island State Park
Client: Texas Parks & Wildlife Department
Design Team: Director: Coleman Coker; Teaching Assistant: Patrick Schoonover; Students: Andrea Becker, Andre Boudreaux, Brooke Burnside, Avignon Greene, Rebecca Kennedy, Whitney Moore, Hugo Reynolds, Sean Reynolds, Joey Rocha, Ui Jun Song, Anthony Vannette
Awards: 2018 ArchDaily International Student Design-Build Award; 2018-2019 Association of Collegiate Schools of Architecture Design-Build Award; 2019 American Institute of Architects, Fort Worth Chapter, Student Merit Award; 2019 City of Galveston Planning and Design Award

One of Texas's most visited state parks, Galveston Island offers access to the beach and bay for more than 145,000 visitors per year.[1] Camping, fishing, and swimming are popular, attracting visitors of all ages for recreational activities paired with TPWD's interpretive programming. The guided nature walk is a popular educational opportunity that explores the park's northern tip, a peninsula with views to the bay, wetlands, and wildlife. Previously, the walking route offered little shade, which was challenging for the many school and scout groups that participate. A good portion of these young people are from low-income and/or inner-city neighborhoods in the Houston area that offer few opportunities to explore nature, who visit the park as part of their middle and high school science courses. "I have a lot of hurdles to get over to make them start to care about this place," explains Lisa Reznicek, park interpreter for Galveston Island State Park. "To get them to some of those higher thoughts, higher concepts—you have to meet their basic needs."[2] With a focus on ecological literacy, Reznicek strives to teach students to respect and value the local environment, and she needed a shaded gathering space to increase student comfort and direct their attention to the water's edge. To better accommodate student groups and the wider public, Texas Parks & Wildlife staff collaborated with Gulf Coast DesignLab in the Summer 2016 semester to design INHABIT, a shade pavilion for teaching, learning, and viewing the coastal landscape.

With the walking itinerary in development through a concurrent park master planning process, TPWD needed a designated meeting point for the beginning and end of the nature walk. Reznicek hoped for an outdoor classroom where groups could gather and sit for casual presentations and group discussions, including an extended orientation talk. TPWD chose a site nestled within eighteen-foot yaupon holly trees sculpted by southwest winds, which frame eastern views to the water and development beyond. TPWD's site selection

A view of the entry side of HABITAT, showing the handicap accessible ramp and recycled concrete gabion wall beyond. © Ava Kikusaki

During their first site visit, INHABIT students gain a better understanding of bay ecology from Galveston Island State Park's nature interpreter. Seen here, they wade through shallow bay waters, while learning about oysters and crab inhabiting the area. © Patrick Schoonover

aimed to situate guests within the park's less-visited wetland landscape, quite a different experience from the more popular beaches on the south side of the park.

Taking cues from the trees, students designed a pavilion with an outstretched wall to draw visitors into the site and shade. The wall, composed of custom-made gabions, extends to the northwest along the yaupons, guiding guests from the nearby parking area toward the structure. Supported by welded steel frames inset with hog wire, the gabions are filled with recycled concrete, spurring discussion about recycling and the impact of materials on the environment. Between the gabions, students designed small nooks and slots to welcome lizards, insects, and other species to the in-between spaces, creating a visual opportunity for onsite teaching. Upon arrival at the pavilion, visitors move off the sand along an accessible entry ramp as they view dense flora through horizontal wood louvers ahead. Disguised by the yaupon holly, the wood platform is lifted eighteen inches off the ground to address rising water levels and provide seating on its edge. As guests reach the end of the gabion wall and turn, views to the east open up as visitors move into the shaded gathering space facing the water's edge. The gabion wall serves as a backdrop for seating, while blocking the western sun from reaching into the pavilion. A seating bench provides space for five to six guests, while the extended deck provides floor space for younger visitors.

Leading up to the build, students spent much of their on-campus, fabrication time on the steel details and welding. Students used computer software to complete a digital analysis of the overhead screen and detail its assembly. They determined the optimal 45-degree angle and spacing for the linear elements to provide shade throughout the day. A small team of talented student welders installed hundreds of custom tabs to support these angled overhead louvers and the horizontal louvers on the south façade. The welded assemblies were then shipped to the coast to be hot-dipped for protection against the harsh, humid climate. Later, a professional welder assisted the students as they installed and connected the structural elements with the custom, pre-assembled components onsite. Students then installed the many wood louvers to shape the wrapping screen and volumetric enclosure.

Since its completion, the project has been well received by users and the design community alike. INHABIT has received local, national, and international design awards and was featured on the Texas Parks & Wildlife television series in a segment titled, "Coastal Parkitecture." This series is available for viewing on Texas PBS channels and TPWD's YouTube channel. Within the episode, Park Interpreter Reznicek reflects on the structure: "This place is going to be highly used—and I think the shade is going to be greatly appreciated in the future," she says. She also shares a message directly with the GCDL students: "Consider this a personal invitation to return to see how this place lives."[3]

Two weeks after construction of INHABIT was finished, Hurricane Harvey hit the Gulf Coast. TPWD concludes the episode with bold, celebratory text: "The Gulf Coast DesignLab's work passed nature's test."[4] Having weathered the storm, INHABIT welcomes three to four thousand K-12 students to the coast each year. The walking itinerary, along with other improvements developed as part of the park master planning process and scheduled for completion in 2022, will connect and reinforce INHABIT's role as a physical and intellectual entry point into environmental education within the Gulf Coast landscape.

—Sarah Gamble

Endnotes

1 Texas Parks & Wildlife Department, Visitation data provided to the author, 22 July 2019.

2 Lisa Reznicek in "Coastal Parkitecture" segment in Season 27 Episode 12 of Texas Parks &Wildlife Television Series, 14:23, August 2017. https://www.pbs.org/video/coastal-parkitecture-bay-trawl-alum-creek-toads-dde5hk/.

3 Lisa Reznicek in "Coastal Parkitecture" segment in Season 27 Episode 12 of Texas Parks &Wildlife Television Series, 14:23, August 2017. https://www.pbs.org/video/coastal-parkitecture-bay-trawl-alum-creek-toads-dde5hk/.

4 "Coastal Parkitecture" segment in Season 27 Episode 12 of Texas Parks & Wildlife Television Series, 3:04, August 2017. https://www.pbs.org/video/coastal-parkitecture-bay-trawl-alum-creek-toads-dde5hk/.

Gaining a deeper understanding of the bay's ecology, INHABIT students pause during their kayak trip to do watercolors of the wetland habitat.

INHABIT students share their initial design ideas with classmates.
© Coleman Coker

Using quick study models, INHABIT students review a few of their many design iterations.
© Andre Boudreaux

Coker and students check construction documents to make last minute adjustments before fabrication begins.
© Patrick Schoonover

To save time working on site, students fabricate parts of INHABIT on campus, which will be shipped to the coast and installed with minimal labor.

INHABIT students install the western shade screen.
© Coleman Coker

INHABIT students drop recycled concrete into the gabion wall. Recycled material was requested by the park rangers for use as an educational talking point when describing the importance of recycling, especially concrete with its high-embodied energy footprint.
© Coleman Coker

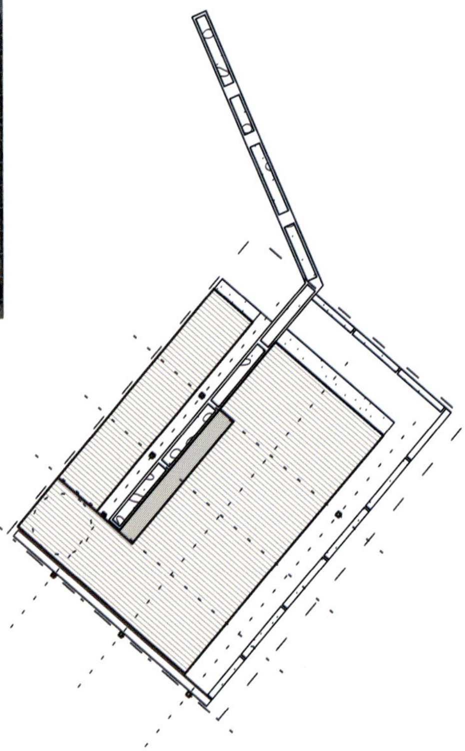

INHABIT students install the overhead shade screen. Using computer modeling programs, the wood member's angles and spacing were designed for maximum protection in the hottest summer months.
© Coleman Coker

Professional fabricators finish up welds on the structural steel frame. INHABIT students completed welding for the gabion wall members.
© Andre Boudreaux

As construction begins to wrap up, a view from the entry side.
© Andre Boudreaux

Visitors stand at the edge of the bay and look back toward the deck of INHABIT.
© Coleman Coker

A visitor enjoys shade from the overhead screens.
© David Schneider

The park's nature interpreter describes the importance of good stewardship practices with a group of high school students from a Houston-area school.
© Avi Kikusaki

A view of INHABIT, looking through the entry opening to the bay beyond.
© Coleman Coker

A finished view of the entry side, showing how the gabion wall bends to guide visitors to the deck observation area.
© Avi Greene

Late fall sunset light
reflects off the southwest
facing sun screens
of OBSERVE.
© Henry Yamamoto

OBSERVE

FALL 2018

Location: Coastal Heritage Preserve, Galveston Island, TX
Client: Artist Boat
Design Team: Director: Coleman Coker; Students: Jacob Castine, Alejandro Davilla, Micayla Garza, Joseph Hernandez, Aaron McMurry, (Fiona) Yee Sang Wong, Zichao Xu
Awards: 2019 City of Galveston Design and Planning Award

Following two successful collaborations, Artist Boat invited the Gulf Coast DesignLab to design OBSERVE, an elevated viewing space and first amenity within the Coastal Heritage Preserve to accommodate the broader public and their interest in birdwatching. Artist Boat, a nonprofit whose mission is "to promote awareness and preservation of coastal margins and the marine environment through the disciplines of the sciences and the arts,"[1] provides environmental education opportunities on the 605-acre preserve, including guided walks and kayak excursions, with a focus on middle and high school students from Houston's inner-city neighborhoods.

In efforts to provide learning opportunities for the broader public, Artist Boat challenged GCDL to design an accessible, elevated observation space to view shore and migratory bird species. For the project, Artist Boat choose a delicate, yet dynamic site on the edge of marshland that is attractive to avian visitors. For those traveling by car or bike, the site is accessible from Stewart Road, a public roadway that runs much of the length of Galveston Island and provides direct access to the bay. Artist Boat wanted the platform to be easily spotted from the road, as guests would be locating the structure by map and without the help of Artist Boat staff or much signage. They also envisioned that the viewing platform would serve as the starting point for a future twenty-minute walking loop moving through the adjacent coastal prairie to offer additional birdwatching opportunities.

Competed in Fall 2018, OBSERVE is a six-foot-wide, two-level observation platform situated less than ten feet from the edge of the salt marsh. Designing for minimal disturbance within the fragile site, GCDL students installed ten concrete piers to support the structure, navigating muddy conditions and a high-water table. The students anticipated seasonal flooding and eventual sea level rise, selecting galvanized steel for the structural frame and pressure-treated pine for the horizontal decks and stairs. The lower viewing platform sits two feet above grade, accessible by a six-foot-wide ramp aligned with the approaching footpath. The upper deck is elevated six feet above grade and is reached by a short set of stairs. From the top, visitors can enjoy distant views to Galveston Bay to the northeast and the Gulf of Mexico to the south, made possible by the platform's

The tall thin form of OBSERVE helps shade birders throughout the day, who line up along the north (right) side of the structure searching for birds in the wetlands beyond. © Henry Yamamoto

OBSERVE students begin their first of site investigation by measuring out potential locations where they might best place their design. © Coleman Coker

elevation and the structure's siting equidistant from the nearby coastlines. In response to Artist Boat's request, GCDL students took extra care in considering the avian perspective from the nearby marsh and distant views for the public approaching by car. Facing the marsh, the northern façade is composed of rhythmic, two-by-four cedar elements, which wrap overhead to create shade. The horizontal elements mask birdwatchers, with staggered apertures offering viewing portals for visitors of varying heights and ages. A portion of the lower deck is designed with accessibility in mind, with ample circulation and viewing space designed for visitors with wheelchairs or other mobility devices. Wider wood elements, measuring two-by-eight, create shelves for steadying binoculars and accommodate seated viewing. Facing the roadway, students placed a series of double-wall polycarbonate (Polygal) panels on the southern facade. The sleek, semi-transparent panels stand out from the surrounding landscape, making the project easy to visually locate. The panels also provide shade from the southern sun and catch changing light throughout the day, light of particular interest at sunset when a warm glow casts across the highly reflective panels.

Several years after the project's completion, OBSERVE alumnus Jacob Castine reflects on these dynamic atmospheric conditions: "The phenomenological conditions, and how they are viewed by the human user versus the natural environment, creates a fascinating dialogue. As a team, we worked to reconcile this all semester."[2] OBSERVE is known to the public as the Edward and Helen Oppenheimer Bird Observatory, noted on Texas Parks & Wildlife website as an officially designated site on the Great Texas Coastal Birding Trail. One of twelve stops on the Trail's Galveston Loop, the area around OBSERVE draws American golden-plovers, whimbrels, long-billed curlews, and upland sandpipers during their seasonal migrations, as well as many of permanently residing shore birds and waterfowl. For human visitors, the observatory is open to the public Monday to Saturday from dawn to dusk.[3]

—Sarah Gamble

Endnotes

1 "About Us," Artist Boat, accessed 15 June 2021. https://www.artistboat.org/about-us/.

2 Jacob Castine (OBSERVE, Fall 2018), Response to GCDL Alumni Questionnaire, 26 October 2021.

3 "Galveston Loop, Upper Texas Coast – Great Texas Coastal Birding Trail," Texas Parks and Wildlife Department, accessed 15 June 2021. https://TPWD.texas.gov/huntwild/wildlife/wildlife-trails/utc/galveston-loop/#utc067.

OBSERVE students at Galveston Island's East Beach are shown birding techniques for basic observing and identification.
© Mary Warwick

OBSERVE students collaborate on design ideas, leading to a project they will build.
© Coleman Coker

OBSERVE students present their final design to client board members for input and approval.
© Henry Yamamoto

Professional steel fabricators are necessary to erect the galvanized steel frame for OBSERVE, since certified welders are required on structures subject to hurricane force winds.
© Coleman Coker

Students infill the galvanized steel frame with structural lumber that is used on the floors and overhead sun screen.
© Coleman Coker

A student works of the steps leading to the upper level; the structure being located toward the middle on Galveston Island, one can see both the ocean and bay from the higher deck.
© Coleman Coker

Students fill in the sunscreen over the upper deck of OBSERVE.
© Coleman Coker

Replace caption: A view from the interior. as students install the southwest facing sun screens.
© Coleman Coker

A view of the south façade, showing a student installing the southwest facing sun screens.
© Coleman Coker

Students install the porous cedar screens, allowing visitors to peer through to the nearby wetlands.
© Coleman Coker

A group of birders look out over the wetlands, hoping to catch a glimpse of birds they don't normally see.
© Henry Yamamoto

A southwest view of OBSERVE.
© Henry Yamamoto

A northeast view of OBSERVE, showing the areas where visitors can look out toward the wetlands beyond.
© Henry Yamamoto

A sunset view of OBSERVE from the street.
© Coleman Coker

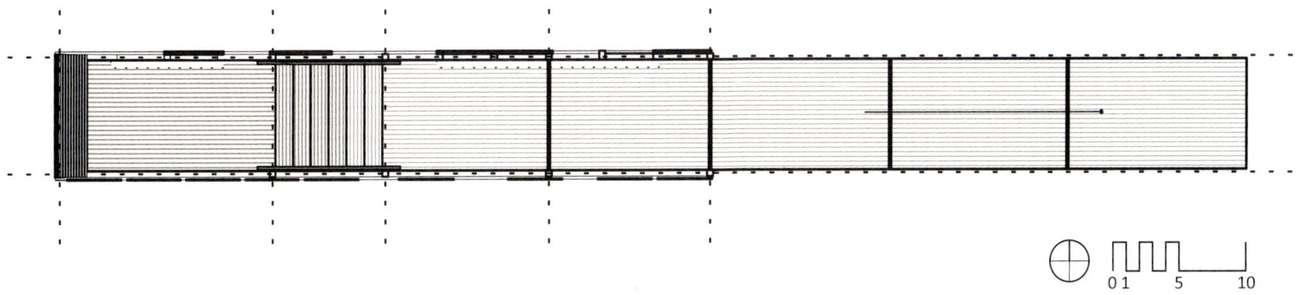

As the sun tracks across the sky, colors of the southwest shading screens change throughout the day.
© Jacob Castine

Students spend the first part of their semester researching local conditions, down to the scale of shells and seaweed, to gain a deeper understanding of place.
© Coleman Coker

CHAPTER 4

A Responsibility to Place

Sarah Gamble

"Most of us think about love as something that happens to us," wrote Mandy Len Catron in her viral 2015 *New York Times* article "To Fall in Love with Anyone, Do This." The piece made famous a 1995 psychology study on human closeness, that, Catron writes, flips most notions of connection because it "assumes that love is an action." Following the original study, Catron suggests asking a friend, partner, or acquaintance thirty-six scripted questions before staring into each other's eyes for four minutes. She claims the intimacy and vulnerability the exercise creates leads to greater familiarity and trust.[1] As we know from personal experience, all relationships begin with a "get to know you" phase, whether that means getting acquainted with a new friend, a place, or a project.

In architectural education and practice, we also enter into relationships—with clients, contexts, and our designs themselves—often engaging with the hope of producing a built work for a particular place. The way this phase is entered into and conducted can tell us a lot about the parties involved, their priorities, and their availability. When successfully undertaken, this initial phase of curiosity centers on open-ended questions, on-the-ground research, and careful observation. Listening deeply, avoiding judgements, and focusing on the needs of others are key to successfully understanding people and place. These discoveries spark greater curiosity, and leave us wanting to know more.

As people rally around the world to address the climate crisis, Catron's approach poses a timely method for design professionals and the development of new ways to "get to know" the places in which we work. The following chapter draws on this model of inquiry to provide the "why" behind our need to act—and shape a call to action of sorts for "how" we can move forward individually and collectively. (References throughout the chapter to we and us are inclusive of the range of built environment design professionals [including my architect self], yet not exclusionary of all others looking to further their positive impact through environmental education and activism.) This call to action is written as much for myself as for my fellow designers, challenging us all to engage with our surroundings in deep and creative ways. It is this act of engagement that will lead to greater knowledge of the natural environment and the transformation of our relationship with it—from generic "space" into meaningful "place" as Christian Norberg-Schulz describes in his writing on phenomenology.[2] Fortunately, from the academy to professional associations, a growing segment of the architectural profession has already begun digging into the "how" and posing their own proposals for change, as they become increasingly concerned about the climate crisis and our relationship with the natural environment. The time has come for designers and educators to rethink design process and the production of built works to engage problems on a magnitude humankind has never faced.

"Climate change is much more visceral on the Gulf Coast than other places. We felt and experienced how harsh it really is."
— Evan Greulich, FLOAT

Environmental Activism by Design posits this idea: Looking to place for inspiration and guidance offers a simple, yet profound, way forward. Cultivating familiarity with and understanding of our environment—both natural and built, local and contextual—has the potential to impact our decisions. Architectural education and practice have focused on manmade constructions (understandably), yet at the same time, largely overlooked human knowledge of the natural environment—and our impact on it. We can start here—intentionally addressing this knowledge gap. The learning (and/or relearning) may be slow. It will take time and effort. And, on the surface, it may seem adverse to our search for efficiency, productivity, and modes of monetization. These efforts will likely face pushback and may be written off as unnecessary or superfluous, and overlooked in favor of priorities perceived as more pressing in the present moment. Rather than an overt shift, we must find nuanced ways to integrate modes of conservation, protection, and appreciation for the natural environment into architectural dialogue and design to overcome societal pressures.

Testing of this slow approach, with place as its guide, is underway by the Gulf Coast DesignLab. The GCDL exhibits how built works, and the process of realizing them, can generate impactful dialogue with communities while raising questions much larger than the architectural projects themselves. GCDL models "how" one approach, which emphasizes environmental education, can be applied and generate a lasting impact on the participating designers and the communities they serve. For built environment professionals, the Gulf Coast DesignLab asks linked questions: Would a more intimate knowledge of the natural environment foster the development of new design paradigms and the production of more informed, sensitive, and beautiful architecture grounded in place? If we had this knowledge, would we be more apt to appreciate and advocate for the natural environment? Could design/architectural practice itself take shape as a form of activism?

Environmental Activism by Design seeks to answer these questions, and the GCDL projects featured here suggest a promising way forward. As they develop their environmental literacy, GCDL student designers subsequently increase their working knowledge and respect for their environment, and therefore, increase their desire to support and protect their surroundings. The Gulf Coast DesignLab showcases how environmental education can be integrated into architectural education to the benefit of design students and the public clients, who utilize the built works they produce. Led by veteran architect and educator Coleman Coker, the GCDL program's studio course fosters an understanding of place and people by prioritizing environmental education as an integral component of design. Students collectively design and realize a built project for a Gulf Coast client, creating spaces where learning continues long after the semester-long course is complete. Expanding upon the "inclusive, pluralistic, and transformative teaching method"[3] that is design-build education, Coker's integration of environmental education into the architecture studio has created a vehicle to push the profession forward—one designer at a time.

Students investigate social systems of commerce and manufacturing, alongside natural ecological systems, to further their understanding of place. © Coleman Coker

STORE students are guided on a wetlands-area walk to learn firsthand about the coastal prairie. © Coleman Coker

The Ethical Imperative

As designers contemplate the ways their work will engage the environmental crisis, it's worthwhile to consider the "why" behind our efforts. Our inherent responsibilities as citizens of the world, paired with our professional ethics, can act as a roadmap for our development as design activists and advocates for the natural environment. In his book *The Ethics of Architecture*, Thomas Fisher argues for the importance of ethics within all facets of architectural design. While the concept of ethics is most often applied within our design professions to contracts, management, and other structured facets of practice, Fisher—professor and former dean of the University of Minnesota School of Architecture, director of the Minnesota Design Center, and thought leader in the field of Public Interest Design—extends this ethical lens to evaluate design approaches and the built environment.[4] He questions the field's emphasis on aesthetics and form-making over its impact on people and the environment. "When people talk about the power of architecture, they frequently refer to its physical characteristics—its space, form, and materials—but its power also lies in its ethical qualities: its ability to provide benefits for people far beyond its immediate users, be they passersby, future occupants, other species, or the public in general."[5] Fisher challenges us to look beyond the immediate specifics of a project, such as its physical characteristics and clients' desires, to consider the broader context of our work and our impact. He emphasizes the ethical imperative to consider surroundings, community, and the general public—all issues of context.[6]

"The natural environment plays a role in every design . . . It's our role as designers to work alongside it."
—Nai'lah Bell, SHIFT

Fisher's ideas extend to the natural environmental and speak to why designers should seek out a more holistic understanding of the places in which we work. As he explains, " 'ecological' psychologists have revealed the sometimes superficial or ineffective ways in which architects have addressed environmental problems, tacking on sustainability as if just one more feature of a building."[7] Fisher highlights how our lack of knowledge has led us to address environmental issues superficially, often under the guise of sustainability, rather than examining the root causes of damage and neglect that plague our natural environment and society. This realization points toward environmental education as a necessary precursor and complement to the profession's focus on sustainability.

As Coker plainly puts it, "Once we begin to know our environment, we will want to nurture and protect it." This premise underpins the work of GCDL and posits that a cultivated respect for our environment will transform our personal practices, fueling advocacy and activism through the architectural design process and the work it shapes. While the status quo approach to sustainability often results in the adding on of eco-friendly features or green materials to otherwise conventional designs, taking the time to learn about and gain respect for the environment can bolster our ability to shape responsive designs from the start—opening the possibility for dramatically different results. Underlying this approach is a form of contextualism, an emphasis of our surroundings that enables us to appropriately, ethically, and aesthetically create a design response for a specific environment or situation. Put into practice, W. G. Clark, well-known design educator and Virginia architect, writes, "We want our things [architecture], like those of the civilizations we admire, to form an allegiance with the land so strong that our existence is seen as an act of adoration, not an act of ruin."[8]

Shaping this "allegiance" requires our intimate knowledge of the land and those who inhabit it. As we cultivate a new (or renewed) respect for the natural environment, we have the ethical responsibility to consider its people, especially those most at risk from the impacts of climate change. As reported by the United Nations High Commissioner for Refugees (UNHCR), "In 2019, weather-related hazards triggered some 24.9 million displacements in 140 countries. Research shows that without ambitious climate action and disaster risk reduction, climate-related disasters could double the number of people requiring humanitarian assistance to over 200 million each year by 2050."[9] Statistics like these may help us to wrap our heads around the magnitude of the problem, but at the same time, distract from the need for local understanding and action. To assist communities, we must become familiar with the "local," its conditions, culture, landscape, building practices, economies, and more to shape place-specific, responsive design solutions. We must apply the "think globally, act locally" mantra and embrace the ethical imperative to address environmental injustices and bolster resiliency through our work.

"The experience gave us a more realistic and harsher perspective on what kind of problems architecture can solve and what kinds it can't."
— Evan Greulich, FLOAT

FLOAT students camp on the beach, an immersive experience to help them better understand the place. © Coleman Coker

Signs of Change

While scientists have long warned of problems created by anthropogenic climate change, the design community, both academic and professional, is showing signs of a collective awakening to our newfound ecological reality—and to our ethical responsibilities to address the climate crisis. Signs of change take a range of forms, including shifts in the priorities of professional organizations, revisions to architectural curriculums, and the chosen recipients of architectural awards. In a 2020 book review for the *Architect's Newspaper*, critic Ian Volner points to evidence of fundamental shifts in the profession and its priorities, writing, "as the decisions of the last four or so Pritzker Prize committees should have made plain, the professional solar system no longer revolves around marquee names hawking signature formal tropes. The Age of the Starchitect is behind us; collaborative and social-minded offices are now in the ascendancy." As we move beyond the illusion of architect as sole author, and often-times hero, toward one that values collaboration and public good, the health of the natural environment and the resiliency of its people become primary concerns for the architectural practitioner. Volner continues, "The discipline is in a very different place than it was ten years ago ... technical innovation, philosophical import, or pure artistic aplomb—all evaluative criteria in good standing until fairly recently—now take a definite backseat to civic virtue."[10]

Like award committees, professional organizations are processing the "why" and making efforts to rally practitioners, educators, and students to address the climate crisis at a broader scale. Established in the United Kingdom, Architects Declare is a nonprofit organization challenging architecture firms to pledge to an eleven-point declaration that recognizes the climate crisis and outlines key actions to address it. One declaration point reads, "advocate for faster change in our industry towards regenerative design practices and a higher governmental funding priority to support this."[11] Now part of the Built Environment Declares network, the architecture-focused organization was founded in May 2019 with commitments from seventeen past winners of the Stirling Prize. By the end of 2019, more than 3,000 firms had signed on through Architects Declare chapters, spanning the globe to a pledge that calls for a paradigm shift in the way architects approach the climate crisis: "The knowledge exists to begin that transformation now, but what has been lacking is collective will. As a sector, we must work together to reshape our approach to architecture and urbanism at the speed and scale the crises demand."[12]

"As a studio, we discussed the painfully obvious lesson that everything we engage with, every building, every article of clothing, food we eat, machine we use, EVERYTHING comes from the Earth. We may be able to adopt a position where the choices we make and the things we create find an equilibrium to the world around us."
— Max Mahaffey, RISE

The American Institute of Architects, the largest professional organization for architects in the United States, is also taking note of the need for leadership and for setting priorities. In March 2019, AIA members at their National Conference on Architecture took a historic vote to adopt the AIA *Resolution for Urgent and Sustained Climate Action*. The resolution aims "to exponentially accelerate the 'decarbonization' of buildings, the building sector, and the built environment."[13] Highlighted in a September 2019 statement titled "Where We Stand: Climate Action," published on the AIA's website, the resolution is one of many actions and efforts intended to guide the organization's membership to embrace their professional responsibilities and "support humanity's collective call to climate action through an unrelenting commitment to sustainable and resilient design."[14]

"Visiting the site over and over showed me that the natural environment is never static, and any changes we, as humans, make have an impact, no matter how small. In order to best protect the environment, we need to understand the potential consequences of our actions."
—Joseph Hernandez, INHABIT

While emphasizing ethics, the AIA's "Where We Stand" statement outlines a range of approaches intended to transform the built environment, including net-zero emission strategies, passive design techniques, low-impact building materials, and renewable energy sources.[15] Evidenced by the 4,860 to 312 passing of the AIA *Resolution for Urgent and Sustained Climate Action*, most architects would agree to the importance of these measures and their integration into built works. However, the "Where We Stand" assessment includes little mention of the education necessary to aid understanding of the broader issues that fuel the climate crisis or the learning designers must do to become more intimately familiar with our environments. As a professional community, do we really need more advice on green building? One could argue that the most pressing need within the architectural profession is guidance and leadership around environmental education that fosters respect for the natural world and encourages new modes of production from beginning to end.

Academics and students are reflecting on the current situation and taking action. In her article for the online venue *Platform,* Anna Czigler explores the changes underway, while reflecting on her own education. "Architectural education, comfortably sitting between theory and innovation, is adapting, but not quickly enough."[16] Citing the research of educator Dr. Corey Seemiller and generational researcher Meghan Grace, Czigler continues, "Generation Z students are not only more aware of the urgency of climate change and attuned to questions of social justice and equality, but more insistent that their work address such concerns, leading them to prefer action over theory. Interests have shifted from form- and space-making to agency-making."[17] Architectural Education Declares, a self-organizing group of architecture students from colleges and universities in the United Kingdom, issued the *Open Letter to the Architecture Community: A Call for Curriculum Change*, which has been signed by over 2,500 individuals, largely students and faculty from European schools. The letter proclaims, "We are concerned that at present our education does not give sufficient weight to the inherently ecological and political basis of architecture."[18] In March 2021, the Architects Climate Action Network, Royal Institute of British Architects, and the Standing Conference of Heads of Schools of Architecture released a climate literacy skills mapping survey to British architecture schools. "The data gathered will be used as a starting point to make sure future generations of architects are equipped with the literacy and most effective tools to safeguard our earth."[19] The Massachusetts Institute of Technology School of Architecture and Planning adopted the *2020 Climate Action Plan,* stating, "The climate crisis is not years or decades ahead, *it is here* ... Acting on climate change is necessary to preserve and further our work ... and should be a focus of our research and teaching. Not acting on climate change will threaten everything that we study and stand for."[20] Since 2019, Columbia University's Temple Hoyne Buell Center for the Study of American Architecture has selected five winners each year for the Course Development Prize in Architecture, Climate, and Society. Explaining their rationale for the prize, the organizers write:

> Education in architecture and urbanism is well positioned creatively and critically to address the exigencies of climate change. However, pedagogical methods that prioritize immediate applicability can come at the expense of teaching and research that explore the sociocultural and ecopolitical dimensions of the crisis. This, in turn, ultimately limits the range of approaches addressing climate change in professional practice.[21]

Together, these moves from practice and academia exemplify the positive steps the profession is taking, starting with pledges and declarations, and (hopefully) leading to transformation within the work of individual practitioners and those in their realm of influence. Yet more guidance is needed. Leaders of our professional organizations, educational institutions, and governments have the opportunity to assess and redirect—considering how to best guide the profession forward.

RISE students listen to a park ranger describe the plight of the highly endangered whooping crane, which came back from the brink of extinction to now winter in the area.
© Coleman Coker

A Proposal

Once we have accepted the "why" behind the need for change, we can look to those putting ideas into practice, such as GDCL, for examples of "how" our individual and collective transformations can take place. The remainder of this chapter outlines simple strategies for furthering environmental education within and through the design process and for fostering new approaches to education and practice. These strategies have been distilled after thoughtful consideration and documentation of the Gulf Coast DesignLab's award-winning projects and conversations with Coker, alumni, and clients, along with complementary research.

Created for the experienced practitioner, the environmental educator, the student, and everyone in between, these strategies are not intended as one-size-fits-all suggestions; nor are they an exhaustive list. They are written with a focus on architectural education and practice, yet they aim to have broader implications for how information and inspiration can be drawn from the environment to foster responsive and place-specific action. The successful implementation of the strategies relies on customization to local conditions, stakeholders, and needs. They are suggested to further a designer's relationship with their surroundings and foster subsequent learning, which then becomes a roadmap for how to move forward with the design process. The approach is one of simplicity, and—aligned with Catron's suggestion—it looks to the needs of others for guidance. If we, as built environment design professionals, can take steps to know our environment more fully, we will be intrinsically motivated to do more—more learning, more conservation, and more appreciation for the place we call home: Planet Earth.

Take time to notice and observe. Rob Walker, in his 2019 book *The Art of Noticing*, explains, "Paying attention is a pretty vital skill for the designer ... cultivating the ability to attend to what others overlook, experiencing 'enchanting reality' as a new and fortuitous gift—is crucial to any creative process."[22] His use of the word "art" implies that the ability to notice can be developed over time and mastered after much practice and training. Walker prescribes active exercises to hone designers' observation muscles, with applications for designers of the built environment and beyond.

Walker's emphasis on intentionality is especially important for the architectural designer, as is the substantial time commitment it requires. Deep listening and looking is a slow process. Time is needed to use our senses to dialogue with the environment. A quick review of rainfall data can't convey the full experience of a rain event: the change in air temperature, the sounds it generates, how the dry ground reacts, where wildlife finds refuge. Reading facts about a whooping crane can't replicate first-hand observation of the birds' flight, eating patterns, interaction with other animals, and preferred resting spots within an architectural site. Observations like these cultivate our familiarity and leave us wanting to know more.

Build up your intuitive knowledge. As we notice and observe, we start to cultivate an intuitive knowledge about the places in which we work. This knowledge takes many forms and is an outcome of slowing down, listening deeply, and absorbing tangible and ephemeral information. While technical data provides great insight, fostering a gut instinct or intuitive sense about what is important and how best to begin the design process is invaluable. If fed broadly, this intuition draws on global and local perspectives, big ideas and detailed specifics, context and site.

"The GCDL design process in the tradition of what we at Artist Boat call eco-art, the integration of ecology and art. The structures are not ecological, but they have to be amenable to being in our ecosystem and respectful of the ecology of the place."
— Karla Klay, Artist Boat

We can look to Josef Albers's writing in *The Interaction of Color* as an analogy for this intuitive knowledge. Albers puts forth a series of introductory color theory exercises that illuminate the impact of the environment on the perception of a color. He emphasizes the impossibility of viewing color in isolation and fosters learning around the interaction and impact of color on other colors. "We are able to hear a single tone. But we almost never (that is, without special devices) see a single color unconnected and unrelated to other colors. Colors present themselves in continuous flux, constantly related to changing neighbors and changing conditions."[23] Rather than studying color from a technical or physiological perspective, such as examining wave lengths or the behavior of our eye, Albers challenges us to train our intuition around color, which he calls an "eye for color."[24] By fostering intuition, rather than technical proficiency, we can gain valuable insights and foster curiosity for environmental education. In beginning architecture studios, for example, the study of shade and shadow and their space-making capabilities through firsthand experiences in shadowed places can be an opportunity to foster students' intuition around directional light. Shaping a gut sense through direct bodily experience lays a foundation for the more technical facets of sun path and angle—and a deeper understanding of the ways designers can shape light for specific situations.

Embrace the environment as a guide for design. Holding a positive view of our environment as a valuable source of information encourages us to embrace and study our surroundings, while acknowledging that architectural design does not occur within a vacuum. Architect Carol Burns describes the role of context in the design process and its potential to be "implemented as a generator, something that provides meaning or content in itself."[25] Viewing project context in this way allows designers to grapple with relevant conditions and concerns. Taking this perspective on the natural environment, the ultimate context of our work, a project's surroundings become the impetus—and likely a focus—of the design project.

Have concern for all living creatures, including people. Cultivating a respect for the environment comes with a concern for all living creatures and the places they call home. We cannot overlook inhabitants of all species, including human stakeholders and the broader community. Most often, our architectural work is in service to people—yet we often prioritize aesthetics, budgets, and material concerns over human factors and, at that same time, overlook concerns for the natural environment. We must engage with clients, stakeholders, users, and the general public to foster concern for all sentient beings and make efforts to understand their needs, impacts, and injustices from their perspectives.

Engaging individuals and communities can be challenging and messy, and it isn't something all designers are trained to do. In the spirit of equity and inclusivity, asking for help is a good idea—because without the insights and trust of project stakeholders, designers can't fully access or respond to all facets of an architectural problem. As Thomas Fisher explains in *The Architecture of Ethics*, "What we chose to ignore says far more about us than what we chose to address, and ignoring equity or sustainability in favor of inventive forms and efficient form-making speaks volumes."[26] Said another way, if we don't engage, we (often times unintentionally) ignore. And these oversights keep us from fulfilling our professional charge to protect "health, safety, and welfare" for all.[27]

Embrace architecture as your medium for action. As designers, we have the power to shape the built environment for public good. Right now, the public needs a built environment that adapts to the climate crisis and contributes to the protection and restoration of the natural world. What we make (or choose not to) is our form of activism. Architecture can broadcast ideas, focus attention, confront injustices, and embrace a position. Architecture can enable us to experience something outside of our ordinary routines or shed light upon a need. Architecture can ask hard questions, and it often requires us to get our hands dirty, in a literal sense, as we collaborate first-hand with site and client.

Be open to collaboration. Collaboration is a central focus of design for the common good and a skill that takes practice. As Volner writes, the architectural profession is only now (more directly) acknowledging that architecture isn't authored by single individuals, but by teams that draw on the skills and expertise of many. Such collections of contributors bring varied experience, generational perspectives, and different backgrounds. Focusing on the natural world, we need help from scientists, researchers, and others who have in-depth understanding of natural systems. We must remain open to collaborations that may have once appeared out-of-the-ordinary, working together with those who have not always been given a seat at the table, such as birdwatchers, public artists, park regulars, and community leaders.

An extraordinary panoramic view of Galveston Bay and the Gulf, just eleven feet above sea level.

A Naturalist and snake expert at the Coastal Heritage Preserve describe wetland area plants to OBSERVE students.
© Coleman Coker

And finally, **seek out opportunities to further environmental education**. As our respect for the natural environment grows, we can continue to further our own knowledge, while embracing the role of advocate and teacher to draw others into the fold. For the architectural professor, inviting environmental educators into the classroom, assigning study of flora and fauna as part of site analysis, and developing in-depth observational exercises can build students' knowledge and foster their respect of the living world. For the firm principal or boss, budgeting for additional and extended site visits, seeking input from local experts, and researching past and current expressions of environmental injustice expose a project team to an expanded range of information with which to shape their designs. For the design student, volunteering for local environmental organizations, spending more time in nature, and seeking out formal learning opportunities are direct means to develop the worldview of an ecologically conscious designer, a perspective that will impact their design process through their careers. For designers at any level, our knowledge of the environment enables us to shape architecture that teaches. Exemplified by the built work of the Gulf Coast DesignLab, architecture, designers' medium for action, can measure flooding depths; orient visitors to the cardinal directions; frame views of native plants; incorporate locally harvested, sustainable materials; and more—shaping learning opportunities for clients, users, and admirers alike.

These high school students are doing prescribed watercolor exercises under the shade and protection of FRAME. Watercolor painting allows these students to better concentrate on what they just saw in their coastal prairie walk and expressing that through rendered image.
© Mary Warwick

MOVE students listen to refugees recently relocated to Texas, who are describing sustainable farming practices from their native Somalia.
© Coleman Coker

Acknowledgments

A portion of this chapter was first published in "Transformation in the Age of Climate Change: Reflecting on the Gulf Coast DesignLab" in *OPEN: 108th ACSA Annual Meeting Proceedings* published in 2020 by ACSA Press.

Endnotes

1 Catron, Mandy Len. "To Fall in Love with Anyone, Do This". *New York Times*, January 9, 2015, https://www.nytimes.com/2015/01/11/fashion/modern-love-to-fall-in-love-with-anyone-do-this.html.
2 Christian Norberg-Schulz, "The Phenomenon of Place." *Architectural Association Quarterly 8*, no. 4: 3-10. 1976.
3 Bryan Bell, Book review of *The Design Build Studio: Crafting Meaningful Work in Architectural Education* (New York: Routledge, 2017).
4 Thomas Fisher, *The Architecture of Ethics* (New York: Routledge, 2018), 6.
5 Thomas Fisher, *The Architecture of Ethics* (New York: Routledge, 2018), 38.
6 Thomas Fisher, *The Architecture of Ethics* (New York: Routledge, 2018), 37-38.
7 Thomas Fisher, *The Architecture of Ethics* (New York: Routledge, 2018), 59-60.
8 W. G. Clark, "Replacement", in Sanda Iliescu, ed., *The Hand and the Soul: Aesthetics and Ethics in Architecture and Art* (London and Charlottesville: The University of Virginia Press), 280.
9 Tim Graynor, "Climate change is the defining crisis of our time and it particularly impacts the displaced," UNHCR: The UN Refugee Agency, 30 November 2020. https://www.unhcr.org/en-us/news/latest/2020/11/5fbf73384/climate-change-defining-crisis-time-particularly-impacts-displaced.html.
10 Ian Volner, "Slip of the Pen," *The Architect's Newspaper*, May 2021: 72.
11 Architects Declare, "US Architects Declare Climate, Justice, and Biodiversity Emergency," accessed 2 February 2022. https://www.architectsdeclare.com/.
12 Architects Declare, "US Architects Declare Climate, Justice, and Biodiversity Emergency," accessed 30 July 2021. https://us.architectsdeclare.com/?fbclid=IwAR2A71ZaCOPRCKOUUNxX32zBRsavaBHO1WCpB8w BH1jPHoCkHQ8fP-g6L4E.
13 Kathleen M. O' Donnell, "AIA's 162nd Annual Meeting Illuminates Ambitious Priorities for the Association's Future," American Institute of Architects, 6 June 2019. https://www.aia.org/articles/6160007-aias-162nd-annual-meeting-illuminates-ambi.
14 American Institute of Architects. "Where We Stand: Climate Change," 16 September 2019. https://www.aia.org/resources/77541-where-we-stand-climate-change.
15 American Institute of Architects. "Where We Stand: Climate Change," 16 September 2019. https://www.aia.org/resources/77541-where-we-stand-climate-change.
16 Czigler, Anna. "Changing the State of Affairs: Making Architectural Education More Engaged," *Platform*, 2 August 2021. https://www.platformspace.net/home/changing-the-state-of-affairs-making-architectural-education-more-engaged.
17 Corey Seemiller and Meghan Grace, "Generation Z: Educating and Engaging the Next Generation of Students," *About Campus* 22, no. 3 (July 2017): 21–26. https://doi.org/10.1002/abc.21293.
18 Architectural Education Declares, "Open Letter to the Architectural Community: A Call for Curriculum Change," accessed 20 October 2021. https://www.architectureeducationdeclares.com.
19 "ACAN Education helps map staff climate literacy in architecture schools," Architects Can // Blog, 28 April 2021, https://www.architectscan.org/post/acan-education-climate-literacy-mapping-architecture-schools.20 David Hsu and Caroline A. Jones, "SA+P Climate Action Plan 2020", Massachusetts Institute of Technology School of Architecture and Planning, 2020, 4. https://dusp.mit.edu/sites/dusp.mit.edu/files/sap_climate_action_plan.pdf.
21 "Course Development Prize in Architecture, Climate Change, and Society," Columbia University's Buell Center website, accessed November 2021, https://power.buellcenter.columbia.edu/initiatives/course-development-prize-architecture-climate-change-and-society.
22 Rob Walker. *The Art of Noticing* (London: Ebury Press, 2019) x.
23 Josef Albers, *Interaction of Color* (New Canaan: Yale University, 1972) 5.
24 Josef Albers, *Interaction of Color* (New Canaan: Yale University, 1972) 1.
25 Carol J. Burns, "On Site: Architectural Preoccupations," in Andrea Kahn, ed., *Drawing, Building, Text: Essays in Architectural Theory* (New York: Princeton Architectural Press, 1991) 147-165.
26 Thomas Fisher, *The Architecture of Ethics* (New York: Routledge, 2018), 206.
27 AIA Office of General Counsel, "2020 Code of Ethics and Professional Conduct," American Institute of Architects, 16 April 2020, 2. https://content.aia.org/sites/default/files/2020-08/2020_Code_of_Ethics.pdf.

All indented quotes from GCDL alumni and clients are drawn from questionaire responses or interviews with the author.

SHIFT opens onto Galveston Bay, providing access and views to visiting K-12 students from area schools.
© Coleman Coker

SHIFT

SUMMER 2019

Location: Kemah, TX, on Galveston Bay
Client: Galveston Bay Foundation
Design Team: Director: Coleman Coker; Teaching Assistant: Andy Garden;
Students: Stephanie Almendares, Daniel Aronson, Nai'lah Bell-Eden, David Burns, Arlene Ellwood, Catherine Kanter, Brandon Lawry, Amaya Lucas, Harrison Marek, Lena Page, Tyler Schuertz, Shelby Taubenkimel, Inci Uckok, Alex Uhlmann, Ariella Yendler

Serving roughly 10,000 students per year, the Galveston Bay Foundation purchased four acres of land in Kemah, Texas, to establish a new headquarters and coastal outpost for their educational, conservation, habitat restoration, and water protection efforts. "Some of the students have experienced going outside and exploring, but most haven't had these outdoor experiences," explains Director of Education Cindy Wilems.[1] With the goal of shaping an accessible and comfortable place for visitors from as far north as College Station, the Foundation choose Kemah, which sits on the western edge of Galveston Bay, a forty-five-minute drive from the center of Houston and five miles from NASA's Johnson Space Center. With a mix of fresh and salt water, the bay is notable for its size in relation to its shallow depth; it is the seventh-largest estuary in the United States, despite reaching an average of only six feet deep. Surrounded by large-acreage residential properties, the Foundation's land sits fifteen feet above the mean water level and is experiencing measurable erosion. The land offered the Foundation an opportunity to continue and expand its activities in the coastal location by welcoming schoolchildren and public officials to engage in environmental education; fostering research and monitoring by citizen scientists and professionals; and expanding conservation and restoration efforts in collaboration with other bay-focused organizations. Planning to develop a new headquarters building in the future, the Foundation invited Summer 2019 Gulf Coast DesignLab students to design the first structure on the site: a pavilion for outdoor environmental education.

While communicating their expansive vision, the Foundation asked GCDL students to design a structure that would be both functional and architecturally inspiring as a reflection of the Foundation's aspirations of making Galveston Bay a better place for the seven million people in the Houston metro area. The Foundation needed an outdoor space to welcome guests, primarily middle and high school students who come in groups of up to seventy-five to take water samples, study flora and fauna, plant sea grasses, and install oyster reefs around the bay's edge. GCDL students took part in many of these planned educational activities during their site visits to better understand future users, experiences that were paired with design review meetings at the Foundation's existing office space in the nearby suburbs. GCDL students' first visit to the site emphasized the fragility of the bay, as they witnessed crews soaking up oil from a recent spill. On subsequent visits to the Gulf Coast, students planted cordgrasses and placed bagged oyster shells to combat erosion, gaining hands-on experience to better understand the project's future users.

Synthesizing these experiences, GCDL students designed SHIFT, a pavilion oriented to the water's edge and the bay beyond. Taking direction from the client on the preferred siting, the pavilion is located within a small clearing of hardwood trees that provide much-needed shade in the late afternoon. "We placed it near a little grove of trees, where there's a little cliff near the water and a great place for birdwatching. Every once in a while, you can see dolphins from there, which is a great teachable moment when you're talking to students," describes Wilems.[2] Responding to the local conditions, an elevated treated pine seating deck is screened by vertical steel louvers along the western and southern edges, directing views to the bay and guiding visitors into the project along a sloping ramp. As visitors move eastward, louvered screens cause their perspective to shift from local to distant and back again as views are modulated by the vertical elements. Constructed of quarter-inch plate steel anticipated to last several decades despite the rusting process, these vertical elements shield views from the surrounding residential properties and from an enclosed steel volume, which currently provides private space for changing wet clothes and was designed to hold two composting toilets planned for the future. To support the solid overhead

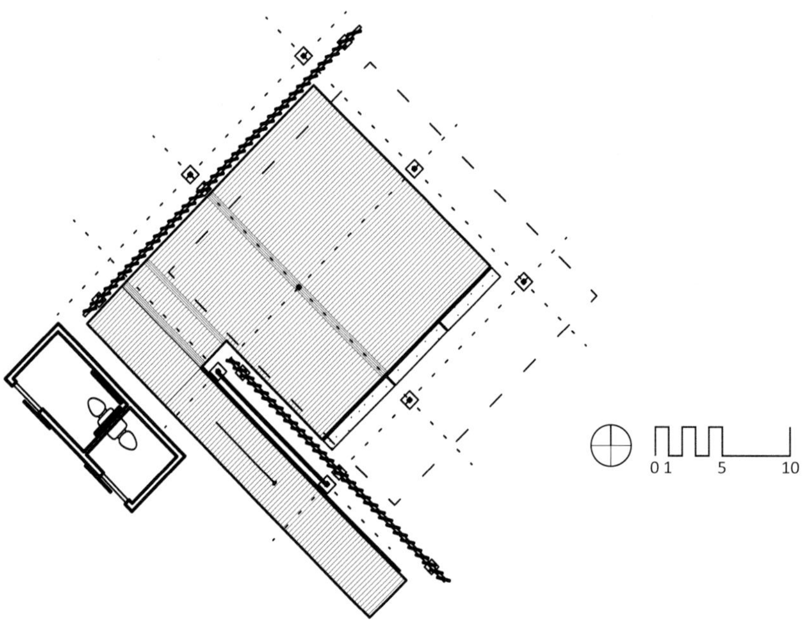

plane, a galvanized steel structure is shifted out of alignment with the seating deck below, extending shade onto the grass beyond. To cap off the deck area, students constructed furniture composed of plate steel and two-by-four cedar, which can easily be moved into the surrounding landscape.

Since the completion of SHIFT, the Foundation is continuing to implement their vision for the organization's headquarters, while working to combat land loss. Around twenty-five feet of the property has eroded into the bay over the past two years, causing the loss of trees and shifting the pavilion that much closer to the water's edge. Heavy storms have exacerbated the problem; in mid-September 2019, Tropical Storm Imelda made landfall about fifty miles southwest of the site, bringing twelve to eighteen inches of total rainfall with heavy winds. To help stabilize their bay edge and dissipate storm surge, the Foundation has built a breakwater about 100 feet out from their property, planted cordgrass, and placed bagged oyster shells. A metal building was constructed to serve as a temporary headquarters and future garage space, as the Foundation raises funds to construct their future home—designed by Kirksey Architecture—and cultivate different biozones with walking paths in the surrounding acreage.

Following a pause caused by the pandemic, visitors returned to the Foundation's property and SHIFT in Fall 2021, with school groups using the pavilion two to four days a week, in addition to the occasional teacher workshop, artist gathering, and Foundation staff happy hour. Wilems reports that the structure serves as a "landing site" for the students and their gear and as infrastructure for educational activities that need tables and shade, such as looking at sea water with a microscope. In addition to meeting practical needs, a visit to SHIFT is an opportunity to experience the fragility of the Gulf Coast firsthand and jumpstart environmental education for students: "Galveston Bay Foundation comes in, a lot of the times, at those beginning stages of environmental literacy. Before we ask students to solve the world's problems—because that's a lot of weight to put on somebody's shoulders—we need to teach them first to know their environment, love their environment, and love where they live."[3]

— Sarah Gamble

Endnotes

1 Cindy Wilems (Galveston Bay Foundation) in discussion with the author, 9 December 2021.
2 Cindy Wilems (Galveston Bay Foundation) in discussion with the author, 9 December 2021.
3 Cindy Wilems (Galveston Bay Foundation) in discussion with the author, 9 December 2021.

Students head to SHIFT from the quarter-mile path that leads from Galveston Bay Foundation's headquarters. © Coleman Coker

Overlooking the water, Galveston Bay Foundation's education director orients SHIFT students by discussing some of the ecological challenges the bay faces due to increasing development, storm erosion, pollution and ever-larger ships entering the Port of Houston. © Henry Yamamoto

SHIFT students researching the Houston Ship Channel to better understand some of the many challenges faced when trying to keep Galveston Bay ecologically viable. © Henry Yamamoto

SHIFT students discuss different design approaches after they have researched local ecological conditions, visited the site, and received input from their stakeholders.
© Coleman Coker

A SHIFT student presents his initial design ideas to fellow students, getting helpful feedback and encouragement.
© Coleman Coker

SHIFT students use drawings, models, and digital renderings to present their design proposal to the director and staff members of the Galveston Bay Foundation.
© Henry Yamamoto

Steel fabricators weld the hot-dipped galvanized, rigid steel frame, designed to accommodate 150 miles per hour hurricane-force winds.
© Coleman Coker

A student welds the privacy screens of SHIFT to their supporting frame.
© Coleman Coker

Once the structural steel has been installed, students begin work on the roof framing.
© Coleman Coker

Students install the floor deck.
© Henry Yamamoto

Students frame the restroom building.
© Coleman Coker

The steel and red cedar furniture was built on campus and shipped to the site toward the end of the project.
© Henry Yamamoto

The privacy screens appear quite open from certain angles and become solid as one moves around the project; foreground restroom structure sheathed in same twelve-inch-wide plate steel as privacy screen fins.
© Coleman Coker

Visitors travel down the handicap accessible ramp toward the water. Note the sheet steel plasma-cut relief map showing Galveston Bay to the right.

To help promote water retention, the Galveston Bay Foundation has a successful outreach program encouraging homeowners to use rain barrels (not shown here) to retain water runoff for their garden and lawn watering. Note the rain chain hanging from roof gutter.
© Coleman Coker

Local middle school students count "nurdles," (small plastic pellets used for plastics manufacturing) commonly found polluting bays and the ocean along the Texas coast.
© Cindy Wilhems

The roof intentionally "shifts" away from the project's privacy screens, leaving room for sunlight with ample shade.
© Coleman Coker

The hot-dipped galvanized metal steel frame intentionally contrasts the naturally rusting cor-ten steel of the privacy screens and restroom structure to the left side of the image.

The project nestles into a stand of hardwoods along its south and west sides, helping block the sun to keep the outdoor classroom cooler in summer.
© Coleman Coker

A large shade screen hovers over the community fire pit with Dash at built-in.
© Coleman Coker

COOP

FALL 2019

Location: High Island, TX
Client: Houston Audubon Society
Design Team: Director: Coleman Coker; Students: Natalie Avellar, Luis Bosquez, Marcella Pastrano, Christian Pena, Draven Pointer, Makayla Ponce, Trenton Sexton, McKenzie Sosa, Iuliia Tambovtseva, Valentina Tambovtseva, Emrehan Tuna, Ruofeng You

A thirty-minute drive east of Galveston, on the Bolivar Peninsula, the Houston Audubon Society operates a Coastal Operations base known as "COOP" in the unincorporated community of High Island. Perched on a salt dome formed by the rising up of a geological layer of salt miles below the earth's surface, it's the highest point on the Gulf Coast between Mexico's Yucatán Peninsula and Mobile, Alabama. High Island's geology and geography create favorable conditions for the extraction of oil, natural gas, and sulfur, and for the growth of trees and scrub important for bird habitat. The area's higher elevation keeps out the periodic flooding that takes place in the surrounding landscapes, allowing for dense flora, intolerant to salt water, to thrive. With available freshwater and wooded terrain attractive to many migrating species, High Island also draws international birdwatchers hoping to witness the spring (mid-March to mid-May) and fall (late September to mid-October) migrations from and to Central and South America. It is most popular in the spring, when exhausted birds stop and rest in the area following their nonstop, 600-mile journey over the Gulf of Mexico. In High Island, the Society manages four sanctuaries interspersed between the private properties that surround the operations base, which provides much needed storage and temporary housing for the society's activities. After working for several years to refurbish existing structures on the property, the Houston Audubon Society challenged the Gulf Coast DesignLab in Fall 2019 to design the base's first new construction, an exterior gathering space with fire circle.

The Houston Audubon Society, incorporated in 1969, describes themselves as "a regional nonprofit conservation, education, and advocacy organization that focuses on protecting the natural environment for birds and people."[1] The Society is also an accredited land trust that owns and manages seventeen nature sanctuaries in five counties totaling 4,121 acres, including the Coastal Operations base. Since 2017, the Society has worked to refurbish existing structures within the base—left behind by the former oil company owners—to create a native grass nursery, bird observation area, refurbished warehouse, bunkhouse, and other facilities to support researchers, their guests, and volunteers who reside in High Island for several days or weeks. In addition, four recreational vehicle (RV) sites were built for environmental educators and volunteers who travel with their own accommodations. The Society saw the need for an exterior space for these visitors to gather alongside local staff and volunteers. Unlike most GCDL projects, which focus on daytime use, the Society envisioned this social space to be used most after the workday and into the night.

Taking its name from a play on words for both the base and a bird enclosure, COOP is an inviting, screened living space with covered fire pit. Adjacent to the RV area, students sited the project to capture full shade from a nearby live oak at the hottest time of day, from mid-afternoon to sunset. Resting on a concrete pad, six-by-six treated pine columns support a minimal, two-by-ten-framed slope roof to create a covered space sized for twelve guests. The bug-screened enclosure protects visitors from the bothersome mosquitos, most active at dusk.

In contrast to the simple geometry of the screened volume, an expressive roof provides shade and coverage to the fire pit area with permanent seating below. The student designers shaped the roof in the form of a hyperbolic paraboloid and lifted it above the enclosure to create verticality within the composition and to contrast the surrounding hardwoods. Thin steel columns support rhythmic two-by-eights to create a porous overhead that allows smoke to waft through. The slant and spacing of the wood elements provide full shade in the summer months. Because of concerns about smoke becoming an annoyance for those visitors in the screened area, the students had originally pushed the fire pit out into the landscape, but in response to client feedback, the final design nestled the fire pit into the screened volume's southern corner. The hyperbolic roof is anchored by a concrete mass, which is also carved to hold the steel-lined fire pit. Bench seating wraps the exterior hearth and is oriented to the southeast, directing views onto a patch of coastal prairie under restoration by the Society.

Since the completion of COOP, the Houston Audubon Society has continued to restore and improve the sanctuaries on High Island, which include the Smith Oaks Bird Sanctuary, S.E. Gast Red Bay Sanctuary, Eubanks Woods Sanctuary, Boy Scout Woods (also known as the Louis B. Smith Bird Sanctuary), and Texas Ornithological Society Hooks Woods. Within the Smith Oaks Sanctuary, the McGovern Canopy Walkway was completed in 2020 to provide visitors with a bird's eye of view of the landscape on 700 feet of elevated boardwalk seventeen feet above the ground. In a follow-up collaboration between the Society and GCDL in Spring 2020, students designed BRIDGE to create a footbridge and walkway between the RV parking area and COOP. The twenty-five-foot-long footbridge was designed to span a small wetland area, while creating an opportunity for birdwatching. BRIDGE students also further developed COOP by constructing moveable tables that offer flexible use. Reflecting on the experience, BRIDGE alumnus Wellington Chew was enthusiastic about the experience, despite the delay in the project's completion until Spring 2021 due to the COVID pandemic. "While we often focus on the large-scale issues facing our society, there are meaningful gains to be made at a much smaller and more accessible scale."[2]

— Sarah Gamble

Endnotes

1 "About Houston Audubon," Houston Audubon, accessed 1 Nov 2022. https://houstonaudubon.org/about/.

2 Wellington Chew (BRIDGE, Spring 2020), Response to GCDL Alumni Questionnaire, 6 October 2021.

A view of the west side as one enters the structure from the RV Camper area. © Coleman Coker

Students ferry across Bolivar Flats while looking toward Galveston and the Bay. © Ava Kikusaki

Students get oriented with the manager of Houston Audubon Society's Coastal Operations Center on the first field trip. © Coleman Coker

A heritage live oak that sits between the new structure and the RV Camper area helps with afternoon shading from the western sun.

After the first field trip and analysis of the site, students review siting of the project.
© Coleman Coker

Students share their individual design ideas with their classmates for the first time.
© Coleman Coker

Students prepare a final model for presenting their design proposal to the clients at Houston Audubon.
© Coleman Coker

Students lay out the area of the building in preparation for pouring the concrete slab.
© Coleman Coker

Steel fabricators install the structural steel that will support the overhead shade screen.
© Coleman Coker

Students begin to frame the outer beams for the enclosed structure.

Students install plywood sheathing over the structural lumber framing for the roof deck.
© Coleman Coker

Students install the multi-ply roof membrane over the plywood roof deck.

Students prepare the structural columns for the insect screen installation.
© Coleman Coker

Students install the frames that will hold the insect screen.
© Ava Kikusaki

Students install the overhead shade screen.
© Coleman Coker

The screened living room is framing complete with the overhead shade screen being applied to the structural frame support system.
© Coleman Coker

The large screen hovers over portions of the screened living room with the fire pit to the east (right in the image).
© Ava Kikusaki

The shade screen hovers low on the south side to block the sun in the hottest summer months.
© Ava Kikusaki

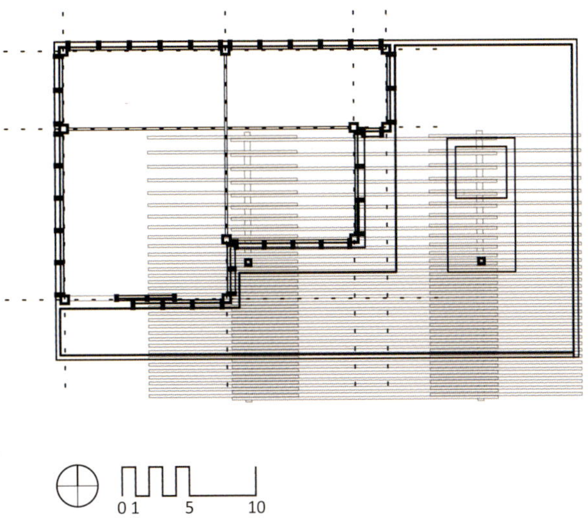

With s'mores and beer, students celebrate the completion of BRIDGE, which was constructed after the outdoor living room structure.
© Ava Kikusaki

Students, including the DUNE studio pictured here, express grave concern about their future and the viability of a healthy planet for all.
© Coleman Coker

CONCLUSION

Ripples of Hope

Coleman Coker

We are living in a truly unique moment, one that gives us reason for hope. There is a sense that change is afoot, that we have awakened to the fact that things cannot go on as they were. We have begun to realize the damage we've done—and are doing—to our only home, taking responsibility for the ecological catastrophe we've wrought. This crisis is finally getting the attention it needs; it is high on the agenda in political debate and is making front-page news on a regular basis. The same is true of the entrenched social inequity that has so stained our nation. Much of the injustice we have witnessed after George Floyd's murder has been unspeakably violent and prejudicially deadly, so much so that it has shaken our nation's foundations. The ongoing discrimination towards people of color and those in less-than-equitable economic conditions can no longer be taken for granted; it must be overcome. These past two years have ripped off ugly societal scabs, exposing that we have been living truly unsustainable lifestyles. Responding in earnest, people who have never done so before are taking to the streets and demanding change, their impatience and frustration transformed into an unstoppable force. There is a sincere feeling that maybe this time it will mean something, that change can occur.

From the couch of homebound isolation, we watch these events unfold to transform the world. In this time of "social distancing," we substitute Zoom calls for constructive work and educate our children through impersonal computer screens. And all the while, many feel rudderless. As prospects of a prosperous future seem to be on hold, there is the awareness that we as a society going forward must do better. We have begun to see that the pandemic is symptomatic of how we've mistreated this planet and the most vulnerable among us. Decades of misuse, unsustainable agricultural habits, over-development, pollution, shifting weather patterns, poverty, and displacement have affected how numerous animals traditionally move about. With their habitats shifting rapidly, they have been forced to overlap with unfamiliar species which they otherwise would never have been in contact with. This has brought about new or morphed cross-species infections, which ultimately spread to us. Exacerbating the spread of diseases is how we trade and eat exotic (and sometimes illegal) animals from compromised habitats. They are sold in crowded, unhealthy markets, perfect environments to transport these new diseases to people. Under these conditions, viruses are allowed to spread rapidly around the world. Most affected are those living in unhealthy, polluted areas—so often the poor—who get little medical attention, making them more susceptible to dietary tract infections and lung disease, which in turn makes them even more susceptible to the ravages of this latest virus. Loss of loved ones; long-haul effects of COVID-19; loss of jobs, homes, and security; long food lines; PPE shortages; self-interest over the collective good; and the inability to act on a national scale are all symptoms of the ongoing collapse of our natural world. They underscore that we only minimally understand how we are impacting this interconnected world on which we rely, while confirming that the COVID-19 plague and the unfolding ecological catastrophe are branches of the same dying tree. And though we may never know the specific cause of this current pandemic, we do know that the consequences of our actions highlight the harm we are doing, not just to the planet, but to ourselves.

With the pandemic having completely overturned the world as we knew it, with our unsustainable lifestyles and societal injustices exposed, this time of upheaval has offered a pause in which we have the opportunity to reflect on how we want to live and where we want to go from here. Many have realized we must do something to change the direction in which we were headed. Many have already begun to bring about much-needed environmental and social change; the groundswell is being felt around the world, particularly by some political and corporate leaders who sense their entrenched way of doing things is over. The adversity many have been facing—and are still grappling with—is motivating many to work more closely together to try to overcome the challenges and explore the possibilities for a better future. A blossoming sense of hope is being felt, but fundamental change is far from assured. Yet, we're beginning to see attitudes and approaches to issues that seemed insurmountable just a few years ago turn a corner. They're not yet collectively large but momentum is there. Change is in the air. We have collective decisions to make, critical ones that will impact all life on this planet for some time. And we have very little time to decide whether we'll confront the challenges ahead and fundamentally change how we live. We have a lot at stake and each of us has a role to play.

"When our work was almost finished, I remember seeing a flock of birds flying, and watching them through the structural frames we'd built, which struck me that it'd be easy for teachers to explain to kids that they're heading north right now, using our building as a reference in the landscape."
—Andrew Stone, FRAME

You may have asked yourself what you can do as just one individual. You may feel that the change needed is so overwhelmingly large—planetary in scope and grand on a human time scale, expanding centuries into the future—that you alone cannot do much. This is indeed true. One person seemingly has little to no impact off-setting the harm of ecological catastrophe or overcoming centuries-old prejudice that has defined who we are. But, one motivated person like you *can* impact the actions of others through the energy you radiate and the enthusiasm you show. It happens every day around the world. Your commitment to change can set off a chain reaction, causing others to do the same. If you think you can't have such an impact, just remember the groundswell of action—millions of people that were and still are—motivated by the actions of one ninth grader in Sweden who stood outside her country's parliament and held a placard announcing she was striking in protest until her government began to take significant action to offset the effects of this ecological crisis. That young woman's single act has transformed the world. No matter how small an action you undertake, it will make a difference.

"We were asked to do some exercises, like write a poem and do a drawing inspired by the location where the structure was going, learning about the place in a poetic way before we started the actual design process—as opposed to just calculating and measuring the sights."
— **Sarah Bensalem, RISE**

If you're not experiencing some level of grief about the unfolding climate crisis then it's only because you've not yet realized the harm we are doing to this earth. If you are alert to what is occurring then your heart must be breaking. Recent studies find that an increasing number of young people, particularly those between the ages of eighteen and twenty-five, suffer from some form of anxiety, sense of hopelessness, fear or anger about the impact that global warming will have on their futures and on the world.[1] Many have little or no faith that government will bring about change, while more express dismay that a large number of their friends and family don't seem to care. Many have trouble putting these emotions into words, but when given the opportunity, they struggle to express a kind of disheartening resignation that no matter what they do, it won't make an appreciable difference. So much so, that a new branch of psychotherapy has emerged to help those suffering from this type of unrest, called eco-anxiety.[2] One of the foundational tools used to help those in this emotional stress is to get them to understand that they can turn they're anxiety into *action*. Acting on our fears is an effective motivator that can bring about change, but acting out of collective optimism accomplishes so much more. And while our individual acts will not amount to much on a global scale, imagine if more of us—with time, many, many more of us—began to make change. Whether small or significant it would not take long for that to add up to something much more. To the point that the eco-anxiety more of us are experiencing about our future is transformed into collective action that changes the direction in which we are currently heading.

Perhaps you are already one of those on the front lines practicing collective optimism that help make people's lives better. Or, you may have a desire to do

This generation of students is more attuned to the fragility of their environment and express a desire to help change the direction in which our western culture is headed, assuring a more hopeful future for all.

Engaging with biologists, environmentalists, master naturalists, and artists, students' GCDL experience offers them a firsthand way of learning that cannot be found through a campus experience alone. The students not only hear from experts, but feel, smell, touch, and listen to the place they work in, offering the opportunity to gain a deeper, bodily knowledge of the wider world.

something but no idea how to begin. To be part of the change, you first must pay attention. Becoming attentive starts by looking, by opening your eyes and seeing the place where you live and how you live in it, and your relative privileges. When you take a walk, ride your bike, or hike on a weekend afternoon, look around with a critical eye to see the change that is taking place. You may have witnessed the leaves falling a little later than they did a few years ago. You may have grasped that snowfall has been less or more, depending on where you live. You may have noticed that birds arrive a little earlier and head south a little sooner. If you've been around for several decades and have been paying attention, you have likely seen weather and animal patterns shifting. And while this may be disconcerting, you may have no idea about what you can do. Nonetheless, you feel you must somehow help bring about change. Start by asking yourself what motivates you. What holds your attention and sustains you sufficiently, something you'll want to invest your time and energy in? What concerns you enough to want to take action? Perhaps it begins with simply caring about what happens to you and your plans for the future. That might be extended to caring about what happens to your loved ones. That concern might even spill over to those you might not know, both now and in the future. Or, it might be something else that you are passionate about: distress over forests that are decreasing worldwide, the increased acidity in the oceans killing off wildlife, the reduction in numbers of the plants and animals you admire. Becoming concerned enough to want to do something is where to begin. Allow it to become something you can identify with: the empathy you may have for the many who are already starving, displaced, and dying; the compassion you hold for the extinction of the many birds and mammals you would admire if only you had the chance; your grief over the scorched trees in the forests where you once hiked; or your anger because the wetlands you once kayaked in are now beyond repair.

For many, places we cherish describe who we are. For many, the places we feel closest to offer a spiritual connection that defines our inner being. Connect the dots and see the larger patterns they all make. Until you come to really *know*—not just with your mind but with your heart—the existential threat that the climate crisis poses, it is only an abstraction, something you believe exists, but nothing

Through what GCDL students have designed and built, it is the hope that the public finds deeper relationship with their outdoor surroundings, and that by doing so, they gain a greater respect for the world around them, leading to a deeper desire to protect and nurture it.
© Coleman Coker

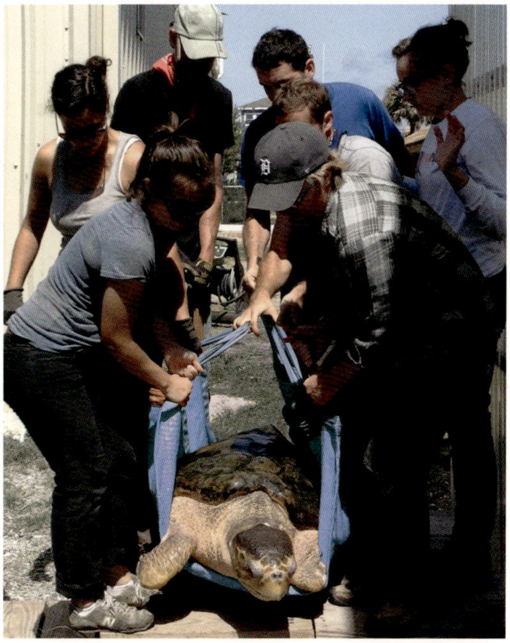

Students' environmental activism takes many forms, here a group from BLIND SIDED relocates a critically injured turtle being treated at the Marine Science Institute in Port Aransas.
© Coleman Coker

Students from BRIDGE look out over Galveston Bay as the moon rises in the eastern sky.
© Coleman Coker

you care enough about to want to change. But, by becoming familiar with the place where you live and finding relationship with those who are in harm's way, only then will you become motivated enough to want to bring about the change needed for a better world.

Commitment might also begin by talking to others in your community, getting their perspectives about the change they have witnessed in their lifetimes. You might ask others how they have been affected by the unfolding ecological crisis and what they are doing about it. You can also read about and listen to what's happening from reputable outlets. Find articles and books that interest you on topics you care about. There are libraries of books that can awaken you to what's happening by well-known writers like Naomi Klein, Barry Lopez, Elizabeth Kolbert, and David Attenborough. And there are too-many-to-count lesser-known knowledgeable writers to draw from. Any of them can change how you see yourself in the world. There are also great documentaries and videos that can open your eyes. Some are box-office successes but most have to be sought out by a little internet research. Get involved in online environmental groups, listen to podcasts. Talk to friends and family who are interested in the same issues. Staying focused on what interests you is the surest way to gain the knowledge you need to do something about the unmatched change that is occurring everywhere. While these won't replace your firsthand outdoor experiences, the main goal is to get up to speed and learn what's a stake. Once you do, you cannot help but be concerned.

"When our Spring 2020 project got put on hold due to COVID, we immediately considered those most impacted, so we put together a fundraiser for a food bank and a group providing PPE, in an incredibly dark and scary time; the sense of purpose this gave me was indescribably important."
—Christie Johnson, BRIDGE

Once that concern takes hold and you feel you're ready, ask yourself, how do I begin to make this world a little better for myself, for others now, and for those who will be here after I'm gone? Once you're willing to invest your time and energy, start small. Don't overwhelm yourself. Do what suits you and the time you have to give. Find out what fits readily into your life, something that will maintain your enthusiasm. It can be a rewarding experience that becomes an expression of who you are. Begin by reaching out to others in your community who are working in ways you find kinship with. They should inspire you, and, in turn, your work will inspire them. They may be like-minded community groups—local or national, civic or religious organizations—that are tackling ecological and social issues in which you're interested. Join forces with them and get to work. What you do doesn't have to be time consuming. It may be an afternoon spent with a group of volunteers cleaning up the river in your community; collecting trash on a Saturday morning beach cleanup; driving a child and her mother living in a fenceline community to the clinic, because the child has a cough; planting saplings in the forest that recently caught fire. Getting involved in local activist groups, advocating for a healthier environment, and particularly for those who live in unhealthy neighborhoods bordering factories, garbage dumps, or polluted streams and bayous are other

Students from the VANAKKAM studio at the Auroville Earth Institute in India learn how to blend soils for making compressed earth block, the primary component for their design of the Bodhidharma School in the Tiruvannamalai region of Tamil Nadu, India.
© Aimée Toledano

Students measure the correct spacing for the structural steel frame on CANOPY at Goose Island State Park.
© Coleman Coker

ways to express your concern. No matter how small a thing you do, remember it will be invaluable. If you do not vote on local, statewide, and national issues, do so. Casting your ballot makes a difference. Voting for candidates who advocate for green policies is far more powerful than deciding to bike to work every day, recycle your trash, give up flying or quit eating meat. Real policy change is powerful and the ballot box is where that change can be made to happen. Democracy works only if enough people who believe in it vote with heartfelt conviction. Voicing your concern through your vote is the one of the surest ways to change public policy, so get involved in the process. If you can afford it, give as you can to the organizations of your choice, and if you can't that's okay, too. There are many ways of "giving," to which your ingenuity will guide you. It takes a few of all these acts from many of us, if we are going to make a difference. Use what you have, rely on the talents you possess, and direct them toward something that can better your life and the lives of others.

"The GCDL helped me understand the environment's vulnerability to our actions, how much damage we have caused and how much we will continue to do if we don't change course."
— Omar McClung, SIMULATE

Making such a commitment doesn't have to feel selfless. To be an effective means for change, motivation *should* begin out of self-interest, since self-preservation no doubt is a primary human driver. You might simply desire a better future for yourself. That hope might then extend to those with whom you are closest. Your love for them might come in the form of your willingness to give a bit of your time and energy for them, for your children and grandchildren, whether you have them now or plan to in the future. The needs of everyone else may not seem as vital as your own; most of us aren't as altruistic as Gandhi or Mother Theresa. But that's all right, for when working to better our lives, and those we cherish, others inevitably benefit, whether they're on the other side of the planet or some of the untold future generations. This is because the problems we face are not local, regional, or even hemispheric; they are global in scope, and for centuries they will affect everyone. We all breathe the same air, drink the same water, eat food from the earth in which it grows, and, regardless of what side of the tracks you and your neighbors live on, we all share in the desire to make a better community in which to live. So, working to improve your local environment, even if the effort you put into it is meant for you, benefits everyone. It's okay to be a bit selfish. In the end, all of us gain from your activism. Contrary to the overused axiom, the whole is not greater than the sum of its parts. Each bit of it is a world of its own, inexorably intertwined with dominions upon dominions, each affecting the other in impactful ways that are sometimes knowable but more often hidden and mysterious, ever-changing and ever-growing. Each of us is one tiny part of that which impacts many others, all parts of equal value. When even the smallest measure is improved, all segments benefit likewise. What you do matters; the actions you take ripple out into the world in untold ways. As Robert F. Kennedy expressed: "Each of us can work to change a small portion of the events (of our world). Each time... a man acts to improve the lot of others... he sends forth a tiny ripple of hope, and crossing each other from a million different centers of energy... those ripples build a current which can sweep down the mightiest walls..."[3] What do you want your future to be? What kind of world do you intend to live in forty, fifty, and sixty years from now? You have the power to shape the future for all the world. Gather your courage and summon the will to become one of those waves of energy.

Shifting our perspectives just a bit, we can begin to appreciate the interrelatedness between the coffee we drink and the rain outside our windows, the trip we make to the mall and the first colors of fall, and how we choose to travel and the health of the ocean we dip our toes into when standing on the beach. Waking ourselves to the world takes a change of focus and a commitment on our part to giving our physical, mental, and heartfelt attention, and to love our neighbors as ourselves. But why not love thy neighbor *more*? This doesn't demand self-abnegation; being open to giving more than you expect of others can compel us to live our lives beyond ourselves and self-interests, so that there is a grander compass by which we are guided. That guidepost is *community*, the community of all living beings, which is precious and to be safeguarded with compassion. Philosopher William James reminds us that, "Science can tell us what exists; but to compare the worths, both of what exists and of what does not exist, we must consult not science, but what Pascal calls our heart... If your heart does not want a world of moral reality, your head will assuredly never make you believe in one."[4] The story we tell is not about how much greenhouse gas is produced each year or whether another great chunk of Antarctica has just broken off into the ocean, but rather a tale about the ethical commitment we are willing to make to one another. It is a human story of love, of caring earnestly for one another, of deeply loving this earth and cherishing it with all our heart. It is about taking that love and turning it into action that will make a difference. Heartfelt compassion inexorably leads to a better world.

"The GCDL was the final puzzle piece for everything else I had learned throughout my architectural education. By seeing a project through its entire lifecycle, I was able to finally understand architectural concepts that had been merely abstract theory before."
—Alex Kelley, RESTORE

This book has spotlighted the work of dedicated design students and the

GCDL students apply metal roof panels to **SUSTAIN**'s Field Station at Crenshaw School for Environmental Studies in Port Bolivar, TX.

Aptly named **FRAME**, the wood frame outside the roofed structure defines planting beds, where different species of coastal prairie grasses are raised. These grasses are grown as a teaching tool for school kids, who will also plant them in the coastal prairie bring restored.

community outreach work they have achieved. Shifting the focus from them as individuals to the broader community of design educators and practitioners and how they might get involved, it must first be underscored that we have the responsibility—the capacity—to blaze a new ethical path. Our discipline engenders the unique skillsets that help us effectively tackle many issues on many scales, even something so overwhelming as the climate crisis. We employ what's come to be called design thinking, nimble skillfulness to successfully respond to outsized problems. As designers, we are pretty good at defining and then finding balanced responses to countless messy issues. Designing a building and getting it built is a monumental undertaking; it requires the combination of technical, social, ecological, and aesthetic capabilities. That effort is seldom a linear process but instead an ever-moving target, full of multiple shifting conditions with unpredictable manifold parts. Designers must have the ability to concurrently address the wishes of our clients; the demands of municipal governments, trade unions, and craftspeople; and the ethical and social needs of the community in which the building is built. We must attend to the comfort and safety of our building's users, not to mention the lasting beauty that we are expected to achieve. We're practiced in grouping multiple issues into manageable assemblages, breaking them down and finding appropriate responses. We're accustomed to planning for unpredictability and acting accordingly. We have learned how to imagine inventively and put that creativity into play. Designers have unique capabilities that can collectively think and act beyond the building norms that have brought us to the edge of calamity that we are facing. By no means comparing what we are capable of to the scale of the problems the world is facing socially and ecologically, we are nonetheless adept at solving complex problems, often for years, sometimes decades, and even longer. Each effort we make, no matter its scale, goes toward repairing the damage. We are at a unique moment in time. We can gather the courage needed to effectively employ our many-faceted skills and respond to the complex social and ecological issues at hand, or we can continue narrowly focusing on issues that are increasingly irrelevant. Dare we use our wealth of imagination and help the human race craft a new ethical foundation that is grounded in compassion, empathy, and inclusion? We have the capability; when will we begin?

Design thinkers can certainly recognize social inequity and environmental injustice; we even contribute our talents to the systems that create them. It takes courage to recognize that no matter how progressive we think we are, implicitly we contribute to inequality and we need to own up to it. We can't change long-practiced prejudicial acts alone, but we have leadership skills and can use them to motivate others, so that they recognize the implicit biases facing minorities and take action to prevent practices such as redlining or placing petrochemical plants or garbage dumps in Black and Brown neighborhoods. Through our professional work and community activism we must insist on respecting each and every person, no matter how unlike us they are. Likewise, the work we do as architects depends on millions of investment dollars, often over the many years it takes to realize our designs. What we propose can make others' lives better but can also bring inequity and environmental harm; we're no small participants in the neo-liberal economic system that operates on the assumption that greed is good. Our participation in that—maybe unknowingly—supports the notion that increased productivity and capital growth greases the wheels of success. Those who suffer most from our tacit inaction to challenge this idea are people of color, the disenfranchised, and the poorest among us. We need to find substantive ways to unhitch ourselves from a financial system designed for those who already have the most. We have the imagination to influence attitudes about how capital wealth can be reshaped.

"GCDL confirmed that there is a place in architecture for good design that serves others, that considers its impact socially as well as environmentally. Where, in school, these priorities often felt 'othered,' GCDL was a very affirming experience."
—Christie Johnson, BRIDGE

As educators who teach design thinking, we can do a much better job when it comes to teaching young designers how to focus on inclusion, just what ethical design can really do, and how to put social equity and environmental justice above all else. We can teach them that getting your building on the cover of *Architectural Record* is not nearly as important as helping a neighborhood get the clean water it deserves. There may not be courses in architecture school that teach students how to be socially compassionate, but we can insist these ideas become part of schools' foundational curricula. We don't typically offer seminars on basic empathy and social responsibility, but we can teach such courses if we choose. Inclusive design thinking helps the future practitioner recognize social inequity and equips them with the power to bring about change. As designers and educators, we can help negotiate the shifting sands of dynamic global change by discovering new ways to teach communities how to help themselves; how they might live sustainably and become more resilient. And by sincerely acknowledging the storm cloud of climate disaster and massive habitat destruction that looms over us all, we can see that effectively responding to it is not an insurmountable task. Through building relationships in the communities where we work, we can teach others to respect themselves and their communities, and to become better stewards of the environment.

These things will not be easy; it will take courage. It will take courage to accept the fact that nothing is more important than teaching our students new ways to think and design that help offset the harshest impacts of climate change, while finding ways to protect those most vulnerable to the effects of dynamic change. It will take the courage to commit to the sea-change that is required, if we really want to prepare students for a future shaped by climate catastrophe. In doing so, we can broaden how we define ourselves as architects and designers. We can expand our communal responsibilities, so that in twenty-five years we hardly recognize what architecture schools have become. They might be reshaped to seamlessly integrate building community relationship, biology, forestry, social science, anthropology, law, and engineering, so that we become generalists instead of the specialists we try to convince ourselves we are not. Architecture schools might begin by asking students to reimagine our societal role. Instead of just designing buildings, we can expand our design horizons to support food growers in urban spaces to eliminate long-haul food distribution. We can help forests rebuild themselves so that they are diverse once again. We can develop programs geared toward community empowerment, self-sustenance, and health. We can design buildings to support kelp and algae farms that will supply their communities. We can design better living systems—what we used to call cities—so they integrate with their local ecologies. We can reshape our teaching methodologies so that they embed students into the communities in which they contribute their design skills, so that their field work focuses on learning to effectively communicate, empathize, and advocate. Designers can, and should, play a role in long term responses to the ecological catastrophe unfolding before our eyes. For each of us, environmental activism by (through) design can mean designing our lives in ways so that we become more fulfilled, so that satisfaction is achieved through helping fulfill the lives of others and making a better world for them. That is the pond in which we might cast a stone that would activate the overlapping ripples of hope, the "million different centers of energy" in which we define who we are. And, in that, there is real reason for hope.

Endnotes

1 Alina Black, "Climate Change Enters the Therapy Room," *The New York Times*, 6 February 2022. https://www.nytimes.com/2022/02/06/health/climate-anxiety-therapy.html (accessed February 7, 2022).

2 ibid

3 Robert F. Kennedy, "Day of Affirmation Address, University of Capetown, South Africa," June 6 1966, https://www.jfklibrary.org/learn/about-jfk/the-kennedy-family/robert-f-kennedy/robert-f-kennedy-speeches/day-of-affirmation-address-university-of-capetown-capetown-south-africa-june-6-1966 (accessed July 8, 2018).

4 William James, *The Will To Believe and Other Essays in Popular Philosophy*, (New York: Dover Publications, 1956) 23.

All indented quotes from GCDL alumni and clients are drawn from questionaire responses or interviews with Sarah Gamble.

An elementary school teacher studies the new aquatic garden at SUSTAIN'S Field Station for Crenshaw School for Environmental Studies in Port Bolivar, TX. Supporters are gathered for the building's dedication.
© Coleman Coker

Middle school students from an Environmental Studies class use **FRAME** within the Coastal Heritage Preserve as their research field station.
© Mary Warwick

Students from the VANAKKAM studio get feedback on their Bodhidharma School design from village elders of Alleyendal in Tamil Nadu, India.
© Aimée Toledano

AFTERWORD

Why Do We Do What We Do?

Katie Swenson

I thought about this question a lot during a three-week trip to the MASS Design Group office in Kigali, Rwanda. Here, we have nearly 70 people working on the design team—architects, landscape architects, engineers, filmmakers, writers, furniture makers, and more. We also started a construction team, called MASS. Build, which has employed more than 2,500 people in the last year. What are the results of the hard work of these talented people? Two new hospitals (one urban, one rural), a new university in Kigali, a center for gorilla research, a new agricultural university, a center for entrepreneurship, and much more. In addition to these tangible, built results, I wonder what this work has meant for the individuals involved? How has the process—as well as the product—influenced the lives of the designers and builders? And how does their motivation to do what they do make a difference in the quality of the work and impact the outcomes?

Soon after graduating with my Master of Architecture in 2000, I joined the Enterprise Rose Fellowship program to work as a designer at a local community development organization in Charlottesville, VA. I was ambitious, but inexperienced. My goal was to integrate best practices in high-quality design and green building into the affordable homes I was charged to design. I turned to both peers and leaders in the field to guide me. One day, I called the office of architect Coleman Coker. I had never met Coleman, but I had admired his work from afar. My impression of his architecture, just from the photos, was that it was grounded in a certain kind of caring. It reflected respect for people, honoring of the natural setting, and elegance of design that wasn't showy, but deeply appealing. They were places I would want to live and would be proud to design.

Now that I have gotten to know Coleman over the past twenty years, it is not a surprise that he took my cold call. He talked me through a couple of design features I was interested in—the metal roofs, in particular—and followed up

Middle school students take part in a water runoff demonstration at the Armand Bayou Nature Center in Houston, TX. Soils containers and enviroscape model were made by students from the SIMULATE studio. © Heather Millar

with some helpful hints. A few years later when I was in Memphis, I stopped by his office to meet him in person. As he came to life with his warm welcome and gentle nature, I understand that his reasons for doing what he does, and the care with which he does it, is manifest in his design.

Why do we do what we do? When I try to understand for myself why I care so deeply about high-quality affordable housing, I trace my inspiration to two things. The first is the beautiful, safe, secure home my parents made for me; the second was volunteering at a shelter for homeless women in high school, where I learned about the horrors of homelessness. The disparity between these two realities was sharp, clarifying for me a passion to work to address the lack of affordable homes for everyone, especially women.

Over the course of my career in design, my "why" has evolved, as I have spent more time with people than at the computer, more time on site than in the office. I began to understand that, for me, cultivating the means for others to pursue their passion was an essential way to address larger, systemic problems like these. I became more interested in lifting the talents of others and helping them pursue their mission in design. The profound benefit of this was getting to know people, first all over the US, and now all over the world.

This kind of exposure is key, and it's certainly the reason why travel is so important in understanding the unique beauty, culture, and challenges of communities around the world. But perhaps equally importantly, it's the people who we meet along the way: the teachers, the mentors, the people we admire, our friends, strangers who become friends. We also learn through doing—through

Students from the YUCATAN studio research salt production at Laguna Rosada, Golfo de México, Yucatan, where sea salt has been made since the time of the Mayans. Students designed a project there for visitors wishing to learn more about the history of sea salt production.

the teaming, through the designing, through the construction, through the pain points.

And so, I found myself in Rwanda, there to develop strategies to support each member of our team. In architecture, we often talk about the buildings, and this team is creating important ones, but our goal at this moment is to invite people to reflect on their aspirations and how they want to grow in their capabilities, careers, and lives.

Asked to reflect on what motivates them, a few of the MASS Design team in the Kigali office said this:

I do what I do because....

> *"I want to be a part of a team that does good in the world."*
> *"I am for people, and I like to see people grow in all aspects. Better designs improve life and experiences."*
> *"I have a duty to serve the nation and beyond."*
> *"I believe in protecting the environment, and using my skills to achieve this gives me purpose."*
> *"It fulfills me, and through it, I can breathe."*

I believe these kinds of personal commitments make a difference. No matter the scale of a challenge we face, whether the design of a small building or working to curb climate change, we accomplish nothing by ourselves. We are always working in teams or within communities. The quality of our relationships has a direct impact on the quality of the work. When we are aligned with our personal passion and our professional mission, we perform better. We make sure it's right. We hunt down the thing that's bothering us, we correct it. But this kind of commitment, I believe, can only be fueled from the inside. Outside forces can affect minor change, but anything worthwhile starts from within. And, when we elevate the individual missions of the people with whom we are working, we do better together. But that also demands courage.

School is one of the places where we expect this kind of personal exposure, development, and transformation. As students head out into the world, the problems they face seem insurmountable. Every person I have met in the field of architecture has a fundamental desire to improve the world through design. But where to begin? How does one turn that lofty idealism into action, into work?

Coleman, Sarah, and the Gulf Coast DesignLab are giving the clues, demonstrating that the classroom can provide the platform for learning, but that nature—the real world, real people, real threats—is the kind of environment where young people can start to challenge themselves to develop their personal commitments. They can get into the messy complexity of life, learn on the job, and not be scared to try. The passion and care of teachers, mentors, community members, peers working in teams—these are the people who help guide us, pick up the phone, welcome us into their lives.

Reflecting on your "why," even as it changes, is a critical tool in bravely taking action. Doing the work of cultural change takes courage. Doing environmental work takes courage. Developing that courage is the learning, it is the lesson. Thank you to Coleman, Sarah, and the students of the Gulf Coast DesignLab for reminding us.

Supporters gather at Artist Boat's Coastal Heritage Preserve to celebrate their new outdoor classroom, FRAME.
© Coleman Coker

Young visitors in East Austin's Boggy Creek Park are drawn to the cast-in-concrete relief map showing the surrounding neighborhood in three-dimensional form.
© Coleman Coker

Students celebrate the completion of PARTING WALLS, located in the native plants area of Corpus Christi Botanical Gardens.
© Wilson Hank

Acknowledgments

Sarah Gamble and Coleman Coker

Many thanks to Coleman Coker for his generosity and patience throughout the making of this book. Through our collaboration, I learned so much about teaching and practice, emerging as a more thoughtful architect and grateful for his influence. Thank you to *Texas Architect* magazine and former editor Aaron Seward for inviting me to write about GCDL's FLOAT in 2017, which jumpstarted this collaboration with Coleman. Thank you to the Gulf Coast DesignLab alumni and clients who shared their thoughts and personal experiences with me through one-on-one interviews and responses to the alumni questionnaire: Natalie Avellar, Nai'lah Bell, Sara Bensalem, Kate Bomar, Victoria Carter, Jacob Castine, Peiwei Chang, Connie Chang, Wellington Chew, Arlene Ellwood, Justin Fluery, Andy Garden, Susie Gibson, Evan Gruelich, Jaclyn Hensy, Joseph Hernandez, Tj Hinojosa, Hannah Ivanci, Christie Johnson, Thomas Johnston, Alex Kelley, Karla Klay, Laura Marley Lancaster, Joshua Leger, Max Mahaffey, Omar McClung, Aaron McMurry, Whitney Peper, Draven Pointer, David Schneider, Andrew Stone, Iuliia Tambovtseva, Nieve Tierney, Claire Townley, Tristan Walker, Charlie Weber, Fiona Wong, and the several contributors who preferred to remain anonymous.

Thank you to the University of Florida College of Design, Construction, and Planning Dean Chimay Anumba and Associate Dean for Research and Strategic Initiatives Margaret Portillo for their support, including subvention funds and financial support for graduate student research. Thank you to my current and former faculty colleagues at the UF and UT Austin architecture schools for their support and encouragement, with special appreciation to UF director (and former directors) David Rifkind, Frank Bosworth, and Jason Alread; UF faculty Martin Gundersen, Nina Hofer, Donna Cohen, and Jeff Carney; and UT Austin faculty Nichole Wiedemann and Judith Birdsong. Thank you to UF graduate research assistant Carly Walker for her dedication and attention to detail in processing through the countless interviews, questionnaire responses, and other research that fed into this publication. Thank you to editor Heather Corcoran for her insightful feedback and guidance. Thank you to my parents, Chip and Gail; my husband, Jason; and my son, Wyatt, for their continued patience, enthusiasm, and support.

Sarah Gamble

Many thanks to Sarah Gamble for her enthusiasm, energy, reliability, and grant-writing skills that helped make this book possible. In addition to her research and writing, her tireless work of gathering alumni and client quotes about their experiences in the GCDL is greatly appreciated, as is her affinity for deadlines and schedules, which kept me on track. I want to thank my many talented colleagues at the University of Texas at Austin School of Architecture for their ongoing advice and encouragement and former dean Fritz Steiner, who generously offered his much-needed support when the program began. Thank you to the Ruth Carter Stevenson Chair in the Art of Architecture for its years of financial support as the program began. Thank you to Dean Michelle Addington, who generously made her Houston Foundation gift available for much of the book's production, as well as the UTSOA's Advisory Council member Tammy Chambless for her generous financial gift that helped fund graduate research assistants' work on the book. I want to recognize the many other donors, volunteers, and in-kind providers who have helped make the students' work possible. Thank you to Professor Kevin Alter, who first invited me to the School of Architecture and has offered his continual support and friendship over these eleven years since. I'd like to also acknowledge Professor Michael Benedikt for his always-reliable advice and support on the book and for his years of encouragement, guidance, and friendship.

Many thanks to Tom Fisher and Katie Swenson, not only for their contributing essays but for their long-standing insistence that our profession be more ethical and loving. I need to thank the many stakeholders and clients we have worked with over the years. It goes without saying that without them, the DesignLab would have only been an idea that never came to fruition. I also want to acknowledge Leora Visotzky for her under-the-radar support over the years as well as her keen editorial eye. And to Sarah Wu for her never-ending optimism and the many unsung contributions she has made to our School. Also, Charlie Weber for his initial research and graphic advice, to Victoria Carter for her steady graphic hand, Evan Greulich, Max Mahaffey, Kaethe Selkirk, Noah Winkler, Thomas Johnston, April Ng, Whitney Peper, David Schneider and Josh Leger for their assistance and creativeness, as well as the many talented research assistants who helped keep the program running smoothly. Most of all, I want to thank the over three hundred and fifty students who have participated in more than twenty-five Gulf Coast DesignLab projects. While I am listed in the University catalogue as their professor, they will never know what extraordinary teachers they have been for me, giving their time, talent—even sweat and blisters—and willingness to go far beyond what is typically expected in any design studio. Their unswerving perseverance has earned my deepest respect and changed my life's direction. I need to acknowledge the intense beauty and complexity that is the Gulf Coast, a living affirmation that the world is astonishing beyond description and worth our every effort to let it thrive. Without it, the DesignLab would not exist. And to Jay, who always encouraged me to return to others some of what life provided; she lives in my heart.

Coleman Coker

Author Bios

Coleman Coker

Coleman Coker, RA, is the Professor of Practice at the University of Texas at Austin School of Architecture and director of the Gulf Coast DesignLab there. He is a Loeb Fellow in Advanced Environmental Studies at Harvard University Graduate School of Design and a Rome Prize recipient from the American Academy in Rome. Coker has practiced architecture for over thirty-five years. He founded buildingstudio in 1999 after a thirteen-year partnership with Samuel Mockbee as Mockbee/Coker Architects.

Thomas Fisher

Thomas Fisher is a Professor in the School of Architecture, Director of the Minnesota Design Center, and former Dean of the College of Design at the University of Minnesota. The former Editorial Director of Progressive Architecture magazine, he has written or edited 11 books, 70 book chapters or introductions, and over 450 articles in professional journals and major publications. He recently completed a book on the post-pandemic world for Routledge, which will be published in 2022.

Sarah Gamble

Sarah Gamble is an Assistant Professor at the University of Florida School of Architecture, following teaching at the University of Texas at Austin from 2011 to 2018. Gamble's academic research focuses on context and how the design process is catalyzed by the surrounding environment and designers' understanding of it. Gamble previously served as Architect of the Texas Historical Commission's Main Street Program, Principal at GO collaborative, and Architect at the Austin Community Design and Development Center.

Katie Swenson

Katie Swenson is a Senior Principal of MASS Design Group, an international non-profit architecture firm whose mission is to research, build, and advocate for architecture that promotes justice and human dignity. Katie received the 2022 AIA Award for Public Architecture and is the co-author of *Growing Urban Habitats: Seeking a Housing Development Model* and author of *Design with Love: At Home in America*, and *In Bohemia: A Memoir of Love, Loss and Kindness.*